THE ESSEX FILES

Everything you are about to read is true
apart from the words and their meanings

Mark Gatiss is one quarter of the Perrier Award-winning comedy team The League of Gentlemen. Born in the north east of England of hardy mining stock, he once submitted a painting of the Loch Ness monster to *Vision On* but it was never shown or returned. When he was five, his mam gave him a skull and crossbones pirate hat but Francis Cameron had one just the same and Mark was very upset.

Jeremy Dyson is another quarter of The League of Gentlemen. Born in Leeds of effete accountancy stock, he once sent a letter to *Jim'll Fix It* asking to be a BBC special effects man for a day but it was never read out. Aged eighteen he pretended to have passed his driving test when in fact he had failed. He was eventually caught, shouted at and shamed, and had three points knocked off his licence.

TO BASILDON
AND BEYOND

Jeremy Dyson and Mark Gatiss

First published in Great Britain in 1997 by
Fourth Estate Limited
6 Salem Road
London W2 4BU

10 9 8 7 6 5 4 3 2 1

A catalogue record for this book is available from the
British Library.

ISBN 1-85702-747-7

Photo credits: p45 © Mick Hudson, Redferns Music
Picture Library, p77 © Theodore Wood, Retna Pictures,
p88 & 89 © David McGill, Retna Pictures

Designed and typeset by Blackjacks
Reproduction by Scanners

Printed in Great Britain by Bookcraft (Bath) Ltd, Somerset

for

Jeremy's Grandma Saville

the original Essex Girl

with love

Acknowledgements

We would like to say thank you to (in order of height):

Sarah Such, Clive Priddle, Russell Heron, Steve Pemberton, Reece Shearsmith, Sandy Kirk, Emma Norton, Sara Cooper, Damien Samuels, Peter Davison and all at PBJ Management.

CONTENTS

FOREWORD
BY PETER DAVIDSON

Hello there, reader,

My name is Peter Davidson.

You may remember me as Robert Glenister's brother in *Sink or Swim*, as one of the vets in *All Creatures Great and Small*, or even as that guy out of *Very Peculiar Practice*. But the role of mine that still keeps my postbag overflowing is that of the mysterious traveller in time and space known as Doctor Who from the BBC's hit show *Doctor Who*.

Many of the letters I receive contain queries about the mysteries of the universe. Their authors make the basic mistake of confusing me with the character I played and expect me to provide them with answers. This of course I cannot do. And I'll tell you what the real mystery is – why nobody writes to me about my other roles. What's wrong with the odd postcard about *Holding the Fort* or *Love for Lydia*? Even a question about writing the theme tune for *Button Moon* would be a blessing (or a *Mixed Blessing* – I did that as well) but no, it's 'Doctor Who, I saw a mysterious cigar-shaped object in the sky. What could it be?' or 'Doctor Who, my house seems to be built on a site possessed by some unimaginably destructive evil, can you help?' or even 'Tristan, my sister seems to be playing host to an ancient Sumarian daemon called Buggeba. Should I call the police?' It's madness. What's wrong with people?

Anyway, if you're inclined towards that kind of nonsense you'll probably like this book, so do me a favour, buy it, and stop bothering me.

God bless,

Peter

INTRODUCTION

There are more things in Heaven and Earth, Horatio,
Than are dreamt of in your philosophy.

Hamlet, Act One, Scene Five – William Shakespeare.

The Cosmos is not silent or sane. It whispers; it dreams; it
communes with all aspects of our psyches in a daily inter-
locution of magic that never ceases.

Memories, Dreams, Reflections – Carl Jung.

People are people so why should it be, you and I should
get along so aw-ful-y?

'People Are People' off
'Construction Time Again' – *Depeche Mode.*

The universe is undoubtedly a stranger and more bewildering place than we have been led to believe. Many of us are familiar with tales of bizarre phenomena from far off times and places – mysterious happenings such as the disappearance of the Dutch Clipper, the *Margot Leadbetter*, – which vanished unaccountably, leaving its crew bobbing in the sea still eating their breakfasts. These stories may seem acceptable to us because of their distance both geographical or temporal. But what of unexplained events closer to home? Somehow they seem less likely. The world each of us wakes to every day, is, after all, an ordinary place. What unsolved mysteries can possibly lurk in a country such as ours, with its Kwik Saves and its Arndale Centres, its Little Chefs and pub quizzes? You would be surprised, for we are now able to exclusively reveal that our own country, the United Kingdom, contains the locus of all that is most

Note the astonishing similarity between President John F. Kennedy and the outline of the county of Essex.

mysterious on Planet Earth. Incredible as it may seem this region of mystery is contained within eastern England in the deceptively benign shape of the county of Essex.

We, the authors, would never have stumbled upon this unexpected truth, were it not for a series of seemingly unconnected events. Somehow they served to point us in the direction of a dark and enigmatic realm which lay concealed just below the seemingly ordinary surface of our everyday world.

Our investigations began innocuously enough whilst researching the distinctly unsupernatural book, *No Better After All These Years – The Syd Little Story*. Syd's comedy partner, Eddie Large, began talking of his time spent touring the working-men's clubs of Essex. Quick-tempered Eddie – a well-known collector of all things curious – recalled that every theatrical digs in which he stayed seemed to have a story all of its own. 'It was incredible,' said Eddie. 'Everywhere I went people told me peculiar stories, tales of spectral apparitions, people with mysterious powers and strange objects seen in the sky. I wanted to write a book about it myself but I was too busy developing a new routine based around my impressions of Deputy Dawg, Cliff Richard and Jimmy Savile starting their cars in the morning.'

Popular T.V. comic Syd Little, enjoys a laugh in his local church.

We too shared Eddie's love of the curious and unusual and since we were travelling south the following week we thought we would investigate some of the sites he spoke of, purely for our own amusement.

We may have thought no more of Eddie's unusual testimony were it not for an inexplicable encounter of our own whilst driving to London on the A127. Returning from a visit to one of the locations spoken of by the *Noel's House Party* regular we noticed we were being followed by a black Ford Mondeo. It drew closer and closer to our rear, attempting to dazzle us with its customized lanterns, trying to drive us off the road. It followed us for nearly thirty miles, making us change our route many times. The vehicle finally left us as we crossed the county border. It seemed that someone didn't want us in Essex.

This disturbing event was followed by the unexpected appearance of a sealed brown envelope delivered anonymously to the authors' shared caravan at Primrose Valley, Filey. The dossier within was written by one Laptop Carey, a former hairdresser employed by Essex County Council. Carey had discovered a covert department hidden in a room behind the Office of Fair Trading, devoted to the collation and documentation of strange incidents. He had smuggled out copies of the files contained therein – each one covering a different phenomenon encountered somewhere in the county – over a period of many years, and was offering the material to us in the hope that we would bring the information to the world at large.

Medium Morris Tarzan producing ectoplasm from his mouth – one of Essex's many unsolved mysteries.

How or why Carey had decided that we should be his mouthpiece remained obscure, but what was clear was that if the information in the files was true, then Essex may indeed be the fulcrum of all that is bizarre and strange in the world. We felt we had a duty to investigate further. We abandoned the manuscript we were writing and started work on a new – and more important – book.

As we began our own investigations in earnest more startling information came to light. Carey had implied that when viewed from the air the county of Essex might reveal even more. Study of aerial photographs and maps at first seemed to reveal nothing more than the shape of a pool of sick. But refusing to accept this we looked again. It was now clear that we were seeing the profile of assassinated US president John Fitzgerald Kennedy. Or TV personality Carol Smillie.

If the former were the case the implications were potentially devastating. Could we throw new light onto the mystery of Kennedy's assassination and its attendant conspiracy theories? Could the patterns of strange phenomena which were beginning to emerge from the landscape of the county have some incredible connection with the Dallas shooting? Were extraterrestrial forces at work? What was the enigma of the Harlow Nightie? What really happened within the Wivenhoe Triangle? And what terrifying secrets were contained hidden within the lyrics of Basildon-born band Depeche Mode?

By examining in detail each of the amazing stories Laptop Carey had discovered we hoped to be able to reveal the fantastic structure which might underlie them all. We knew this might be a dangerous endeavour, taking us deep into the heart of Britain's strangest county, but we owed it to Carey – who seemed to have paid the ultimate price for his discoveries and vanished without trace – and to ourselves who had nearly met our own fate on a lonely stretch of the A127 five miles from Basildon.

Several years ago it is unlikely anyone would have been interested in our story, but now, thankfully, the climate of official indifference and obfuscation has been challenged. Minds have been opened by the success of TV series such as *Dark Skies*, Michael Aspel's *Strange But True Encounters* and *Scooby Doo*. At times what you read may seem incredible to believe but that is for you to decide. One thing we can assure you – the county of Essex is an even stranger place than you can possibly imagine. An unparalled vortex of the weird, a zone of the unusual and a damn sight more interesting than Syd Little.

So read on and enjoy this most important book. And if you've found it in someone else's toilet go and buy your own copy.

Jeremy Dyson and Mark Gatiss,
Primrose Valley, Filey
Autumn 1997

FILE 1

THE MOST HAUNTED BUILDING IN ESSEX – 'GOSSIP'S' IN ROMFORD

By moonlight's glow as whyte as ice
was seen by all with rule and dice
a lady fair but pale – o pale!
standing fast upon the stair
her skin like as parchment
her hair same, and sparse
a steel pike poking from out her arse

Gossips,
Romford –
Haunt of
the Dead?

So wrote sixteenth-century Essex scribe William 'Wee Willy' Withey about the notorious house of pleasure with a dark reputation that was to have a devastating effect on the life of publican Gary Stears. Had he known of its history he may never have taken over the property which turned out to be the most haunted building in the county – Gossip's Nitespot, Romford.

'When my dad bought the place it was a real dump. It looked like a bomb had hit it. This was – what? – 1945. It was a pub. Pretty run-down. Me dad thought "Yeah I can do something with this." With hindsight perhaps he should've twigged there was something strange about the place because of its name – "The Dominion of Lucifer, Lord of Misrule" – but he didn't think anything of it at the time.'

Essex scribe
Wee Willy
Withey

Big Fat Ghost

The building was in fact even older than Stears Snr supposed. It had originally been constructed as an alms house for fat women in 1452 and its association with the supernatural began only a year later. Bess Thighs – a notably large lady of the parish – became stuck in a window-frame and was pinched to death by a gang of cruel children. It was soon said that Bess Thighs still walked the cramped confines of the alms house in spirit-form and her manifestations were not confined to sightings. Large quantities of food started to go missing as evinced by this extract from the journals of local clergyman Abbot Dainty:

> *'a chille morn ande I sette me downe to eatte, the houre beinge close to noone: Pon inspectione I founde the cupboarde bare. A hamme, an orange, a quaile, two dates, an egge, three digestives, a cowwe, syrup, and summe grapes, all of which I had espiede onlye the nite before had vanish'd. I was like to think Big Bess was aboute her business.'*

The haunting became so serious that the alms house was closed. It remained empty for almost thirty years, locals being too scared to go near lest they hear the ghostly belching late at night.

Garry Stears finds something terrible in his toilet

Stinky Spooks

Gary Stears takes up the story. 'I'd always been aware there was something funny about the club – even when I was little. Strange writing – often obscene – would appear on the toilet walls overnight. And there was this terrible smell coming from the urinals. It was always worse after a busy evening in the club – I think the activity must have disturbed the spirits. It also troubled the ladies' loo which became blocked with some kind of ectoplasm. The plumber said it was sanitary towels but I know different.'

Extract from the Carey Papers

The records of local historian and chronicler of the strange, Laptop Carey, reveal the sordid history of the building.

X 1490. The disused alms house was opened as Essex's first sauna and massage parlour – 'Sensaytionnes' – but the technology was too primitive to allow it to function properly and a group of Guildsmen perished on opening night when they were placed in a room that was simply on fire rather than full of steam. Ten died and the ghost of Bess Thighs now had company.

X 1540. The almost derelict building was converted into a brothel and gaming house by the infamous Naughty Michael – Essex's most famous alchemist and exotic dancer. There was much talk of doings with the devil, sacrifices and bizarre sexual rituals as this extract from the journals of noted Romford clergyman and diarist the Reverend Geoffrey Stilts shows:

'Tuesday. Another night at Naughty Mikes. Christ. There was this one bird. Stack'd like London Bridge with a jewel box you could get King Edward's crown in. And what she could do with a steel pikestaff would make your eyes water. Played Nine Men's Morris, followed by cards then drank the blood of eleven virgin choristers. All in all a good night out.'

Naughty Michael, one of the sauciest men in Essex's history.

X 1738. Extensively rebuilt, the property was reopened as a tavern by an ambitious group of homosexual highwaymen known as the League of Nancies. Despite the building's ghostly reputation it prospered for a time as a safe house for all manner of scoundrels, ne'er-do-wells and sailors of the Greek persuasion. But the idyll was not to last as the revenue men's suspicions were aroused by the premises' name – The Great Pink Cock.

X 1895. Aware of the building's evil reputation decadent aristocrat Lord Percy Ssledge purchased the land and reopened it in the guise of a gentlemen's club. Its membership were dedicated to the worship of the devil apart from alternate Saturdays when the site doubled as a synagogue. Lord Percy eventually disappeared in mysterious circumstances. Some say he was consumed by the vengeful spirit of Big Bess Thighs, others that he met a nice Jewish girl, moved to Manchester and settled down.

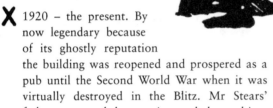

X 1920 – the present. By now legendary because of its ghostly reputation the building was reopened and prospered as a pub until the Second World War when it was virtually destroyed in the Blitz. Mr Stears'

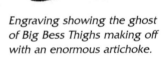

Engraving showing the ghost of Big Bess Thighs making off with an enormous artichoke.

father renovated the premises and changed its name to Brief Encounter's, one of a planned chain of Romford nightclubs inspired by the films of Sir David Lean.

Nitespot of Fear

Gary Stears remembers: 'I'd spent a lot of my childhood in dad's clubs – Oliver Twist's, Summer Madness's, In Which We Serve's – they was all happy, nice places. But 'Encounter's was troubled – what the bible calls a leprous house. I had hoped that renaming it Gossip's would help drive the ghosts away, but I was wrong.'

So frightened was Gary Stears that he called in Larry Rice, the county's leading ghost hunter and exorcist, to see if anything could be done about the atmosphere of evil. Rice was less than impressed claiming that everything Stears had observed was 'a load of bollocks' and caused purely by natural phenomena. He also accused Stears of being motivated by nothing more than the desire for free publicity and to appear on *Newsroom South East*. But extensive investigation by the authors of this book has raised the following questions which demand answers.

X What are the mysterious grunting and moanings heard in Gossip's car park after dark.

X What causes the unexplained cold spot felt near the fire escape by the cigarette machine especially between the months December to February.

Rice: Bollocks

X What evil force inspires outbursts of violence amongst the young clientele of Gossip's, often accompanied by the ghostly cry 'leave it Ian, it ain't worth it'.

X What poltergeist activity lies behind the regular smashing of the glass in the bus shelter near Gossip's entrance.

X What lies behind the pools of ectoplasmic fluid – often foul-smelling and full of vegetable matter – that appear apparently of their own accord outside the nightclub's entrance.

We are certain that Big Bess Thighs and her unholy brethren do not lie quiet in their graves and they undoubtedly form one tile in the mosaic of fear spread across the county of Essex.

FILE 2
'BIG' LEE VINCENT –
THE ESSEX URI GELLER

'Alright darlin', 'everything a pound a scoop, it's good stuff this, not shit, 'ere mush get your fingers out of those avocados. Do you mind? Jesus!'

"Big" Lee Vincent – one step ahead of his Israeli counterpart?

These are the words of 'Big' Lee Vincent in his more worldly guise of a Canvey Island market trader and entrepreneur. But this mundane exterior hides an altogether more extraordinary personality – that of 'Amazing' 'Big' Lee Vincent – Essex's answer to Uri Geller.

Wayward Romanies Kissy and Kyrle Vincent seen here on their way to a knife-sharpening convention

Just an Ordinary Boy

For one who was to lead such an incredible life, Lee's childhood was perfectly normal. The eighth son of Romany peddlers Kissy and Kyrle Vincent, Lee was just an ordinary boy who scrumped apples, played football in the park and helped to cut up the bodies of local villains – an off-shoot of his dad's knife-sharpening business.

'It was just your average Canvey Island boyhood really,' says Lee with a wry grin. 'Family was very close, everyone always poppin' in and out. Never locked the door. The house was always full of laughter...and screaming. Terrible screaming.'

Lee's mysterious talent – or 'blessing' as he likes to call it – first became apparent when the young lad accompanied his father on his rounds. While Kyrle Vincent was busy sharpening away, Lee's astonishing mind was having a powerful effect on items of customers' cutlery.

Former client, Janet Coats, remembers: 'I'd leave little Lee playing in the kitchen while his old gypsy dad sharpened my bread knives. It was only when I came back I noticed something strange had happened to my spoons and forks. They'd disappeared.' When she confronted Kyrle Vincent the astonishing truth was revealed.

The Power of Teletranscombobulation

It seemed that Lee had inherited the power of teletranscombobulation – the ability to reduce matter to its most basic form. With his mind alone he was able to literally make things disappear.

As Lee grew so his powers increased and other customers began to notice the mysterious disappearances. Consumer durables seemed particularly susceptible to the phenomenon with TVs, car radios and music centres dissolved into the ether. His fame spread, and Lee – now fifteen years old and known as 'Big' Lee – became something of a local celebrity appearing on *Look Romford* and on several radio phone-ins. During the latter Lee would make astonishing predictions about teletranscombobulations to come.

Lee can make TVs, camcorders... even cars disappear with his amazing power of teletranscombobulation – are they in fact being transported to another dimension?

His technique involved asking callers to provide certain information about themselves so he could build a full psychic profile, including details of age, occupation, marital status and when they would be going on holiday leaving their premises vacant. Sure enough his predictions would prove uncannily accurate with entire houses stripped bare by the sheer force of Lee's mind.

It was then that the man who would prove to be Lee's psychic mentor and guide through the pathways of the spiritual in our material realm – publicist and pornographer Derek Glass.

Tits and Glass

With his chain of 'specialist' bookshops and successful publications such as *Busters, Gash* and *Old Age Arse,* Glass was already a familiar figure in the showbiz world to which he now sought to introduce Lee.

'I'd seen the lad on the box. Knew what he was capable of. I thought he could do a lot better for himself with his talent. I imagined him teletranscombobulating in the homes of the rich and famous, in palaces, in Hollywood even. I wanted to be the man to guide him. A facilitator if you like.'

'How' on Earth

A dazzling round of parties and engagements followed, each one saw an amazing teletranscombobulation more spectacular than the last. Popular TV presenter Jack Hargreaves recounts what happened to him: 'It was the wrap party for the third series of *Out of Town*. I was entertaining friends with some whittling when this big rough lad came in the room. He said "Ere, grandad, I'll show you a trick." At that time I owned a lovely yellow Rolls-Royce Silver Cloud and it was parked right outside the studio. Lee asked us all to close our eyes and count to three hundred. Whilst my eyes were closed I felt this – I don't know, let's call it a psychic force – rifling through my pockets. When we opened our eyes again it was incredible. My keys, the lad and the car were gone. As Bunty (and later Marion), Fred, John and I used to say, "How?"'

Mungy Pittz

Ruud Awakening

But storm clouds were gathering. Dutch psychic investigator and arch-sceptic Abram Ruud had heard tell of Lee's exploits and was determined to expose him as a charlatan. The Dutchman was known as a fearless debunker of psychic phenomena. It was he who had seen through the notorious possession of Mungy Pittz a thirteen-year-old African girl who claimed to be able to produce ectoplasm at will. The discovery of four hundred tins of Campbell's mushroom soup in her bedroom established Ruud's reputation.

Ruud caught the ferry to England specifically to lay down a challenge to Lee to prove his skills, by demonstrating them under laboratory conditions. Lee's initial response was one of detached indifference – in conversation he was known to refer to Ruud as 'that Dutch cunt' – and was content to enjoy the trappings which his fame had bought him. But Ruud's insistence began to rattle Lee's stoic calm. Derek Glass attempted to mediate, thinking he could buy off the sceptic with a bottle of Bell's and a life-time's subscription to his latest publication *Very Big Women*. Ruud was unimpressed. He again threw down the gauntlet suggesting that Lee teletranscombobulate in a strictly controlled environment some random items of Ruud's choosing – say the four hundred tins of Campbell's mushroom soup given to him by Mungy Pittz's grateful parents.

Dutch Courage

Although Lee and Derek presented a composed front they were reportedly shaken by the allegation that many of the items that Lee had teletranscombobulated were actually to be found in a lock-up garage in Upminster. It transpired, however, that while Derek acknowledged the lock-up's existence it merely represented another facet of Lee's extraordinary powers: the ability to telerecombobulate the earlier tele-discombobulations. 'It's obvious innit? The things he can dissolve into the air well he just puts 'em back together. Something like that.'

Double Dutch? Sceptic Abraam Ruud was less than convinced by 'Big' Lee's powers.

Mysteriously, less than twenty-four hours before Ruud's requested demonstration, Lee devastatingly proved the sceptic wrong by making the Dutchman himself vanish. For two days the world watched and waited. Then, amazingly, Ruud was teletranscombobulated in the same garage in Upminster. Pale, bleeding and shaken he refused to talk about his baffling experience and the time spent in 'the beyond'. He went back to Amsterdam that same evening never to return. Although much press attention focused on a recorded telephone conversation between Ruud and Lee in which the latter was alleged to have said 'Disappear? I'll make you fucking disappear you Edam-chewing, windmill-fucking, wanker. Is that what you want? Hm? Is it?', Lee's reputation survived intact.

'Big' Lee Today

Not long after this however, the dream began to unravel. A row with Derek Glass over the teletranscombobulation of Derek's then girlfriend – former Miss Westcliff, Karla Fowler – into Lee's bed led to an acrimonious split.

Lee began to grow tired of the limelight and the pressures his fame brought. Although he remains reticent about this part of his life it seems that he sought spiritual guidance with several local police officers, particularly after a gruelling telediscombobulation which led to the disappearance of a fleet of Securicor vans.

He decided to retire and invest his savings in a fruit-and-veg stall. He remains a popular figure however in local pubs and clubs where his amazing skills are still in evidence. Publican Gerry Shipman commented: 'Lee's a great lad. He'll amaze everyone with his psychic powers. I've known cheque books, credit cards even the entire contents of the till disappear into the ether. Last Christmas he even helped me out by telerecombobulating a brand new Toshiba with nicam digital sound under the tree. Thing about Lee is he's always there for you...for a price.'

FILE 3

PICNIC AT COBBLER'S MEDE ROCK

The brooding landscape of south-west Essex, linked with a wealth of ancient mysteries provides a dramatic backdrop for a strange, and still puzzling, disappearance.

Girls at Corringham College revising for their annual exam in fighting.

St Valentine's Day 1919 dawned sunny and bright in the village of Stanford-Le-Hope on the outskirts of Thurrock. It was the day of the annual outing of Corringham College, a well-appointed girls' school with a reputation for strict discipline run by Presbyterian minister the Reverend Babar Capote and his wife Janice.

Early that morning, a party of school-girls and teachers together with the Capotes' pet monkeys drove out with a picnic to nearby beauty spot Cobbler's Mede Lake, famous for its distinctive rock which poked out of the middle of the water. It all started out as a cheerful occasion – but by the end of the day six of the group had disappeared in mysterious circumstances: what is more two of the girls, two adults and a monkey were never to be seen again.

Reverend Babar Capote and Janice.

This unusual story has become a *cause célèbre*, the subject of countless theories, much speculation and an article in *Women's Realm*. But like many historical mysteries the Cobbler's Mede Rock affair is perhaps not all it seems.

A Journey into Mystery

According to the legend the party set out in a hired coach to the lake. Although it was only 500 yards from the school the Capotes' monkeys enjoyed the bouncing sensation of riding in the vehicle and so they were indulged by their owners who made the coach driver circle the school grounds many times before finally leaving through the front gates to travel the short distance to the water's edge.

Riddle of the Rock

Cobbler's Mede Rock is an unusual geographical formation. Part sandstone, part accumulated rubbish, the rock rises majestically from the water to a height of almost seven feet terminating in a little mound of discarded Christmas trees, left there every year by local residents. Today it also sports several old mattresses and a supermarket trolley.

The party comprised twenty-two pupils from the college, and two teachers. These were Greta Onion, a middle-aged spinster who taught animal husbandry, and Mlle Marie de Moulinex, who taught French and fighting, and had a pathological fear of robins. The only other adult member of

Aerial photo revealing the brooding majesty of Cobbler's Mede Rock

the party was Bentley McGraw, the coachmaster from the local livery stables. McGraw had no official connection with the school but 'enjoyed the company of teenage girls'. McGraw also took charge of Tinkle and Jools, the two chimpanzees, feeding them segments of tangerine at regular intervals throughout the day.

What Happened at the Lake?

Nothing happened at the lake, it happened at the rock.

What Happened at the Rock?

At around two p.m. some of the senior girls asked permission to swim out and explore the rock. The two teachers were reluctant at first but Bentley McGraw persuaded them it would be quite safe with two conditions:

1. That he accompanied them.
2. That the girls removed some of their garments before entering the water to avoid the risk of drowning.

The four pupils – Irma Bunt, Rosa Klebbe, Fatima Blush and a girl remembered simply as Stumpy were all aged seventeen and known to be sensible. The girls were warned to be careful and to look out for robins by Mlle de Moulinex.

At about three thirty the chimps became fractious. Mlle de Moulinex searched for some tangerines but realised that McGraw had taken the supply with him. Realising the time she became anxious about her charges and went to consult with Miss Onion. It was at this point she realised that her fellow teacher had gone missing too – she must have followed the group out to the rock.

The Vanishing Picnickers

At first irritated, then concerned the anguished French mistress organised a party of pupils and monkeys to find the missing group, only to discover that now Tinkle, too, had vanished. Some of the girls swam out across the water only to return with conflicting reports. The first there, Jilly Masterson, claimed to have heard noises – soft moaning and grunting – but the next group who searched every inch of the rock found nothing but a piece of tangerine skin and an empty jar of palm oil. There was no trace of the missing picnickers.

Red Indian Tracker Black Squirrel.

The Aftermath

For nearly two hours the distressed party searched for their missing members although they took a fifteen-minute break for tea at four forty-five. Then at about five thirty Irma Bunt scrambled onto the water's edge. She was screaming hysterically and could tell her interrogators nothing apart from the time of day and the best way to cook scrambled eggs.

Later in the day when interviewed by Reverend Capote and a local policeman she revealed that she had passed Miss Onion in the water, with Tinkle the monkey clinging to her back. Even worse was the fact that the normally prim spinster was improperly dressed, paddling frantically, wearing only her drawers and an inflatable bathing-ring. Irma could offer no more information.

The search continued for several days. The Capotes were naturally particularly frantic. Tinkle had never been apart from Jools for that length of time before. On the Thursday following the picnic the police brought in a Red Indian tracker called Black Squirrel in the hope that he might have been able to find some clue they had missed. Given a pair of Miss Onion's drawers to sniff he retired to the rock for several minutes only to return a little flushed but with no new evidence.

Eventually the search was reluctantly abandoned. Irma Bunt was unable to shed further light on what had taken place, and the Capotes bought a new monkey.

What Really Happened that Afternoon?

There has been much speculation over the years as to what really took place that Valentine's Day. Some believe that the girls may have been spirited away by aliens – Cobbler's Mede Rock is a distinctive landmark and the pile of Christmas trees may have acted as a beacon that drew curious intergalactic visitors to the lake. Mlle de Moulinex had her own theory that the party were eaten by robins

Rice: 'Shite'

although this gained little credence with police at the time. Another account states that Bentley McGraw was a white-slave trader who sold the girls to a visiting Sheikh, throwing in the monkey as part of the deal. Supernatural expert Larry Rice, who conducted his own retrospective investigation into the events at Cobbler's Mede Rock, concluded that the whole story was 'a load of shite', and that, although some of the girls had been a little late back that afternoon, the only mystery was what exactly McGraw got up to with four teenage girls, an old maid and a monkey.

Picnic at Cobbler's Mede Rock

In 1975, Essex-born film maker Tinto Fist made a disturbing and atmospheric movie of the events of that fateful afternoon called *Picnic at Cobbler's Mede Rock*. Starring Googie Withers, Bernie Winters and a young Lesley Joseph the film achieved international acclaim for its haunting mood, understated narrative and surprisingly upbeat musical numbers.

Other Essex-based Vanishings

✘ In 1974 the Little Chef on the A12 between Galleywood and Howe Green was found mysteriously abandoned by staff and customers. Some tables still carried warm pancakes with a sachet of maple syrup next to them, unopened.

✘ In September 1991 Kathy Foster, Nathalie Duffy and Tracey West went out for a night at Chaplin's Fun Pub in Saffron Waldon. When they returned home in the early hours of the following morning all three girls discovered that their knickers had mysteriously disappeared. No trace of the panties has been found to this day.

✘ On February 14th, 1997, Dickie Driver – a publican from South Woodham – woke up one morning to find his wife Michelle missing from his bed. What's more most of her clothes and a large suitcase had vanished too. 'I couldn't understand it,' he told investigators at the time. 'Where could she have got to?' When asked whether he thought the violent arguments the couple used to have, together with the fact she had frequently been seen with an Italian hairdresser called Carlo might have any link with her disappearance, Driver was adamant that there could be 'no connection'.

FILE 4

SPRING-HEELED CHRIS – THE TERROR OF BRENTWOOD

Artist's impression of Spring-Heeled Chris – the terror of Brentwood.

The lonely lanes and commons of suburban Essex have been haunted by some terrifying apparitions over the years. There was the Muckingford Horror – a vile creature with the talons and beak of a bird and the body of a PE teacher who reputedly stalked the pastures of Walton Hall Farm. Or the Dirty Lady of Leigh-on-Sea who was said to appear in the gloomy corners of the Golden Egg Café and steal patrons' chips. Or even the Hound of Norsey Wood – an over-sized spectral pitbull whose appearance was said to be a portent that the unfortunate observer would be involved in a fight the following Friday. But there is no spectre more frightening than the weird figure of Spring-Heeled Chris whose mysterious antics troubled the good citizens of Brentwood for more years than they cared to remember. Famous for pouncing upon innocent passers-by, distressing them severely in a number of bizarre ways and then leaping off 'as if his legs were made of springs'.

The Legend of Spring-Heeled Chris

Until recently Spring-Heeled Chris was dismissed as a figure of the imagination – a mere character in Victorian penny dreadfuls or a bogeyman used by mothers as a threat to children caught watching *TFI Friday*. Thomas Chesney-Hawkes in his book *Victorian Bastards* says that Chris is 'just made up' – perhaps the invention of reluctant servants who used stories of encounters with the bouncy wraith to explain why they were late back from the pub.

Author Thomas Chesney-Hawkes seen here demonstrating an Edison Aural-Perambulator, forerunner of the Sony Walkman.

*First edition of
Victorian Bastards*

But Chris was not a character in fiction, folklore or legend. He was real and his attacks were widely reported in the press both in Essex and about the country. Unusually for a Victorian villain he even had his own fan club with bi-monthly newsletter and membership card.

The Early History of Spring-Heeled Chris

Nobody is sure when Chris made his first appearance. There were reports of a stupid-looking jumping man as far back as 1822 although this may have been a sighting of an early member of the Natural Law party. It was not until 1843 that Spring-Heeled Chris became a familiar topic of conversation at both fashionable dinner parties and horrible pubs where poor people went.

On the 12th February that year, the Lord Mayor of Brentwood, Sir James Taylor-Quartet, revealed at a meeting of the town council the contents of a letter he had received the week before. He had withheld it for several days both in the hope of obtaining further information and also because he wanted to study at his leisure the pornographic etchings on the inside of the envelope. The writer of the letter identifed himself only as 'a rude gentleman' and that as the result of a wager 'an individual of the highest rank' had adopted a number of shocking and silly disguises and set out to 'make thirty people wet themselves'. The letter continued to describe how he had already 'succeeded in depriving seven young ladies of their senses' and 'dampening the gussets of several more'.

The Many Guises of Spring-Heeled Chris

In his first incarnation Spring-Heeled Chris was famous for adopting a variety of different forms. These included an enormous baboon with pendulous breasts, a knock-kneed circus clown with live fish in its hooped trousers, an elderly nun with a blue velvet wimple and a thick waxed moustache, a very small

An enormous baboon with pendulous breasts.

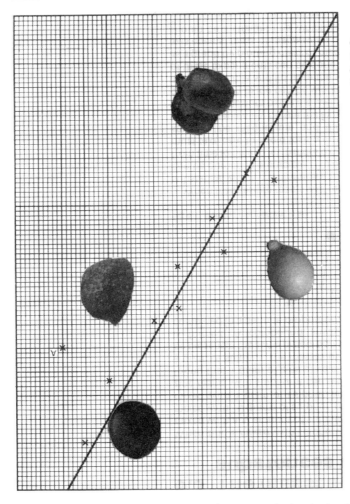

Chart demonstrating the rising incidence of Spring-Heeled Chris's attacks

steam train and a comical purple and white cow – the inspiration incidentally for the Milka chocolate advertising campaign of the early 1990s. Once, in Herongate, a southern district of Brentwood, Chris appeared as a portly town-crier, naked from the waist down, who carried his bell between the cheeks of his arse.

The Attacks of Spring-Heeled Chris

On Wednesday 21st June 1845, nineteen-year-old Lucy Jinglebells replied to a violent ringing of the front doorbell of her parents' home. She opened the front door to reveal a man in a long black cloak which covered him completely from his neck to his feet. He explained that he was a policeman and begged Lucy to fetch him a po because he was 'in desperate need of a wee-wee'. When she suggested that he could come through the house and use their privy the man threw aside his all enveloping cloak revealing a skin-tight oilskin suit decorated with crude paintings of different kinds of fruits. He then suggested that the terrified Lucy might want to 'squeeze his strawberries or fiddle with his plums' and then pulled her towards him discarding a stream of cherry stones which he had concealed in his cheeks into her bonnet. Lucy's screams had attracted the attentions of the piano-tuner who was working in the front room. Seeing what was occurring he slammed the front door in her assailant's face telling him to 'go away'.

Several weeks later Chris tried the same deception at a doctor's house in Upminster a number of miles away, but for some reason the housemaid who had answered the door was suspicious and refused to speak to him. A witness claimed to have spotted a pineapple and several sticks of rhubarb protruding from beneath the 'policeman's' cloak.

Later Sightings of Spring-Heeled Chris

Spring-Heeled Chris's appearances were always intermittent and gaps of many years would go by with nary a squeak from the vaulting maniac. Just when the citizens of Brentwood had forgotten about him he would suddenly emerge again with another weird assault. But after 1862 there were no further reports of any incidents for over a decade until in December 1874 the *Daily Sketch* reported that 'the village of Stock was in a considerable tissy owing to what is known as the Stock Hopping Ghost...a mysterious figure, quite as alarming in appearance as Spring-Heeled Chris who caused members of the past generation to wet themselves'.

The Identity of Spring-Heeled Chris?

There are many theories as to the identity of the original Spring-Heeled Chris. The most likely candidate is Henry de la Poer Voer de Seour Coeur Freur, the

Marquis of Walton-on-Naze who already had a reputation as an infamous prankster from his years at Eton and Oxford (he was a student at neither – he just used to spend time there bothering the children of other noblemen). His sense of humour was notoriously offbeat – once he arranged for all the waiters in a restaurant to be fired and replaced with blind men so he could laugh at them trying to serve soup. One night in 1851, having visited the races, he painted all the old women in the town red without their permission. He and his cronies were each fined three shillings for their decorative stunt.

Later that year, The *West Mersea Herald* reported that:

Henry de la Poer Voer de Seour Coeur Freur – The Marquis of Walton-on-Naze

'The Marquis of Walton-on-Naze passed through this town the other day, standing atop a coach with a number of his associates. In the course of the journey they amused themselves by lobbing live chickens, sharp cutlery and burning hot coals at any unfortunate individual who happened to be standing by the wayside.'

The Times commented on this incident that:

'This lively person is a long time sowing his "wild oats". He is now nearly sixty-two years old.'

The Marquis of Walton-on-Naze's exploits ceased after some time and he became a model of respectability after his death in 1879. His connection to the activities of Spring-Heeled Chris has never been proved although it is known he was very fond of fruit and indeed was reputed to have introduced the guava to the shores of this country after spending time in the tropics as a merchant seaman.

FILE 5

S.H.E. - THE RIDDLE OF SPONTANEOUS HUMAN EXHAUSTION

'The victim sat in a chair, surrounded by empty cans of Carlsberg Special Brew. On the small coffee table in front of him were cartons made of silver foil. Later inspection showed up remains of chicken korma and peshwari naan. An ashtray full of cigarette butts lay on top of the television which was still on although transmission had ceased. The victim was slumped forward and despite the lateness of the hour had made no attempt to go to bed.'

Extract from report on Spontaneous Human Exhaustion produced by Essex Metropolitan University, 1992.

The report opposite concerns the strange case of Eddie Stepney, discovered by his girlfriend Yasmin apparently overcome by unexplained tiredness. Eddie's night had seemed perfectly ordinary. He had been down the pub with a group of friends and after a boisterous evening had returned home to watch highlights of the final of the Embassy World Darts contest. When he hadn't come to bed by four a.m., Yasmin went downstairs to investigate and found her partner completely incapacitated. 'I just couldn't understand it,' she recalls. 'It was Bobby George's big comeback and he slept right through it. I came in and found him snoring like a pig. It was completely inexplicable.'

This phenomenon, known as Spontaneous Human Exhaustion or S.H.E is by no means a recent occurance with examples recorded around the whole of England – it once affected an entire audience attending a recording of BBC's *How Do They Do That?* – but there is an abnormal concentration of this bizarre phenomenon in the county of Essex.

"I could not be arsed"

Eddie Stepney – slept through George.

S.H.E.

The affliction is distinguished by a number of recurring characteristics:

 It is always highly localised; those surrounding the victim are often entirely unaffected. For example in the case of retired fitter Freddy Ratcliffe. He fell into a mysteriously deep sleep on a sofa one Sunday afternoon, whilst his son-in-law, wife and daughter remained completely awake watching the film *Ice Station Zebra*.

S.H.E. makes an appearance in Charles Dickens's little-read, Essex-based novel *Daniel Liquorice*. The protagonists Mr Dimple and Mr Waveychilde had instructed their employee Jabez Fite to spend the afternoon tending to the affairs of their late client Mrs Belsize. Fite had been alert and apparently eager to work. They return to find an altogether different state of affairs.

Entering the room after great circumlocution, the pair were struck by a oppressive atmosphere as of unaired clothes.

'Ho there' cried Dimple moving to draw back the heavy drapes.
'What! Asleep?' Waveychilde frowned and took out his watch from his waistcoat pocket.

'It's not yet three...Hi Jabez. Get up there, get up I say.' But the figure on the couch made no movement and the blanket drawn across it spoke of a terrible indiscretion.

Oh but an awful sight was this! For although the sun was still high in the sky a mysterious torpor had seized the unfortunate Fite. And worse, Mrs Belsize's papers lay untouched on the mantel. Dimple threw up his hands. Waveychilde prodded the clerk with his stick.

'Fite! You rascal. What is the meaning of this?'

'Oh Mr Waveychilde' cried the clerk in horror. 'I am so wery sorry about the papers, but you see sir, I just couldn't be arsed.'

X There are often tell-tale material signs that a victim has succumbed to S.H.E. These include: sticky, dusty deposits in the corner of the victim's eyes, amounts of drool escaping from the victim's mouth, and empty bottles or cans containing traces of alcoholic beverage.

X Although S.H.E. seems to paralyse the entire human frame almost instantaneously upon onset, some parts of the body remain mysteriously active. For example the fingers are still able to flick the ash off a cigarette, or the channel change buttons on a TV remote control

The Vengeance of S.H.E.

The following case studies exhibit all the classic signs that an S.H.E. has taken place:

Beverley Myers, a thirty-two-year-old mother of four found her whole life bent out of shape by the horrors of S.H.E. Husband Ron comments:

'Beverley was full of beans when we first got married – always the life and soul. But when what I know now to be Spontaneous Human Exhaustion afflicted her, she became a dowdy drudge. I'd be at work all day and when I came back I expected things, you know, conjugal things, but she never seemed up to it. It was weird. All she had to do was look after the four kids, see to

Beverley Myers – harried mother of three

my mother, keep the house tidy, have my meal on for me when I got back and work afternoons as a doctor's receptionist. When I heard about S.H.E on James Whale's radio show I knew this had to be the explanation.'

Anthony Nicholls was a groundsman and caretaker at St Luke's Catholic boys' school in Foulness. Every Sunday his wife Madge would invite her family round for a big lunch. After each meal she requested that her husband 'at least do the bloody dishes'. But strangely Mr Nicholls was never able to comply, for whenever his wife returned to remind him of his duties she would find him struck down by what could only be an attack of SHE. 'I'd go in the sitting room and he would already be half asleep. When I repeated my request he would give an odd scowl, shake his head and laugh as if I'd asked the earth of him, before closing his eyes.'

Groundsman Anthony Nicholls.

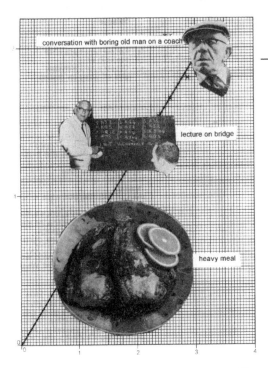

conversation with boring old man on a coach

lecture on bridge

heavy meal

Chart revealing events likely to produce incidents of S.H.E.

S.H.E. May Be The Face I Can't Forget

Although the phenomenon of Spontaneous Human Exhaustion is undoubtedly mysterious the theories offered in explanation are often prosaic:

1. The sudden fatigue characteristic of S.H.E is caused by a large cloud of hydrogen peroxide – a result of too many cheap perms – drifting across the county.

2. Given the hectic pace of modern life, people are just tired.

3. Supernatural expert Larry Rice has a theory of his own. 'Well they're just lazy buggers aren't they,' he says.

Rice: Buggers

Whatever the explanations the authors can certainly testify to the phenomenon's existence. During the writing of this book they were often gripped by incidents of S.H.E, making it difficult to work, especially during the summer when it was nice outside.

FILE 6

THE ESSEX CODE – THE FUTURE FORETOLD (IN EIGHTIES POP)

'I see great success not only for "No Good (Start the Dance)" but also for its follow-ups. However you must beware the one called Keith. He will bring much difficulty for you in late 1996.'

Extract from a letter received by Liam Howlett of The Prodigy in early 1994.

Ritz Krakas – Number one Israeli Depeche Mode fan.

Basildon's nicest young lads – The Prodigy

996 had been a remarkable year for Essex-based techno-rave outfit The Prodigy. They had already enjoyed two number one hits with frantic dance numbers 'Firestarter' and 'Breathe' as well as signing to Madonna's Maverick record label. But the truly amazing thing was not that a band which featured a ginger-haired fool who looked like Russ Abbot's idea of a punk rocker could be taken seriously; rather it was the fact that an Israeli mathematician called Ritz Krakas had foreseen The Prodigy's massive success nearly two years earlier and had sent his detailed predictions in a letter to the boys, which even warned of a *Top of the Pops* ban because of dancer Keith's scary appearance. And Krakas had other, more amazing prophecies not only for Liam, Keith, Leeroy and Maxim but for the rest of the world, although the source of the academic's uncanny prescience would cost him his mind.

Puttin' on the Ritz

The story begins a long way away from Mr Krakas's book-lined study in Tel Aviv, thousands of miles away in fact in the somewhat less rarefied environment of 'Sweeneys' – a rock venue in Basildon, circa 1980 where four young men with long-crimped fringes and thin leather ties had gathered to make a new kind of pop music. Vince Clarke, Dave Gahan, Andrew Fletcher and Martin Gore were all united by an electro-pop dream. Their name: Depeche Mode – literally 'fast fashion'. Amongst the sparse crowd at that first gig, was young maths student

Ritz Krakas who accidentally found himself there after misreading the name of the third band on the bill and thinking the venue was a kosher deli.

Krakas's journal recalls: 'Chopped Herring had finished their set and I'd realised my mistake. I was getting pretty restless and hungry when these young men came on stage and beguiled me with their deceptively simple synthesized beat. Amongst the tunes they played was an early version of "See You" and I just knew that I'd be "seeing them" again.' In fact so keen did Krakas become that he

formed the very first Depeche Mode fan club and became a popular figure with the band members themselves. Speaking today from his Los Angeles hideaway frontman Dave Gahan fondly recalls: 'Who?...Oh yeah.'

Special He-Brew

After early chart success Depeche Mode left their humble Essex roots to achieve international acclaim, veering towards the darker side of rock. And Ritz Krakas was with them every step of the way. 'I'd lived and breathed the Depeche dream for nigh on ten years but when I got the offer of a mathematics chair at Tel Aviv Metropolitan University I knew I had to start a "New Life" myself.'

Krakas returned to his homeland where his academic career flourished. For a while distracted by Venn diagrams and quantum mechanics his sojourn in Essex seemed to belong to another time. But one day, gripped by nostalgia for his former life he began a project to translate all of Depeche Mode's lyrics into Hebrew and put the resulting database onto the Internet where other Semitic enthusiasts of the Basildon boys could access it. 'At first I thought I'd just do one or two tracks but then I became obsessed, taking on the whole first album. After all the boys remind us that "Everything Counts" in large amounts.'

It was when he was halfway through this exacting task that Ritz Krakas made an extraordinary discovery. He found that if he highlighted every fifth letter in the first two verses of the song 'Dreaming of Me' it spelt out the words Upstairs at Eric's.

Depeche Code

'I was astonished,' said Krakas. 'Here was the name of the debut album by Vince Clarke's spin off group Yazoo. And yet it was encoded – in Hebrew – in the words of a song recorded two years before Vince split from his fellow Depechers.' And that wasn't all. Krakas found that if he transcribed the lyrics of the whole song as one block of Hebrew text he could also make out the words 'big-boned', 'jazz singer' and 'Alison Moyet' crossing Clarke's name, another uncannily accurate prediction of the songwriter's musical destiny.

Startled, Krakas wondered whether this new theory was applicable to other songs in the Depeche canon. 'I thought I'd have a go at "I Just Can't Get Enough". My hand trembled as I began to transcribe the lyrics of the top-ten hit wondering what secrets the Hebrew characters would reveal. I couldn't believe my eyes. I didn't want to start any "Blasphemous Rumours" but I was beginning to wonder if I'd found my own "Personal Jesus".'

In point of fact the lyrics seem to have foretold not only the future of Depeche Mode but also of other Essex-based musicians and outfits. For example the title track 'Speak and Spell' when deciphered by Krakas yielded the words 'Cars', 'Gary', 'Aeroplane', 'Numan', 'Tory' and 'Cunt'. 'I was sure this couldn't just be coincidence,' he explains.

Krakas's journal continues: 'I knew I was really onto something when I decoded "New Life" and found that it contained an incredibly detailed account of Blur's hollow victory over Oasis when their "Country House" pipped "Roll With It" to the number one slot in the summer of 1995, only to see their Manchester rivals sweep to ascendancy later that year. It was remarkable.'

Blancmange – Gravel voiced singer.

'Enoch' – Powell

If Ritz Krakas's work had only contained prophecies about certain Essex-based musicians it would have been extraordinary enough, but the Depeche Code had more surprises to reveal. When the mathemetician turned his attention to the second album 'A Broken Frame' he was startled to discover that the foretellings were veering away from the Basildon boys' county of origin to speak of the fates of others.

Sensing things were getting a little too big for him, Krakas made contact with top US defence department code-breaker Buckminster Powell who was at first sceptical.

'I've come across this kind of thing before' explains Powell. 'In 1985 I was involved with the debunking of a document that claimed to have found details of all ten seasons of *Hawaii Five O* chronicled within the Book of Enoch. I set out to disprove Krakas's assertions but when I found the name of Stephen Luscombe – the gravel-voiced singer with top early eighties electro-outfit Blancmange – hidden in the Hebrew translation of "Get the Balance Right" I knew this was different.'

It now appeared that the Code somehow predicted the entire history of British electro-pop. Powell explains: '"It's Called a Heart" contained an elaborate cryptogram revealing the ultimate fate of Andy McCluskey and Paul Humphreys of Orchestral Manoeuvres in the Dark, whilst "Love in Itself" spoke of the failure of Human League spin-off the British Electric Foundation and the phoenix-like rise from its ashes of Heaven 17, even detailing their ultimate, unlikely collaboration with Tina Turner.'

In an excited frenzy the American code-breaker set to work transcribing as many of the songs as he could, scarcely able to believe the details he was uncovering. 'When I translated "Shake the Disease" I found within it an incredible year-by-year account of the history of proto-electro-rockers Ultravox including details of their work with German super-producer Connie Planck, their move from Island records to Chrysalis, John Foxx's solo career and their eventual number two success with the classic "Vienna". I mean it even mentioned how they would be denied the number one slot by Joe Dolce's "Shaddup a ya Face". It was truly amazing.'

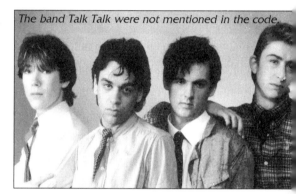

The band Talk Talk were not mentioned in the code.

Krakas goes Crackers

By now Ritz Krakas was speechless. 'I felt like throwing a "Black Celebration". I couldn't "Shake the Disease". The whole thing was like a "Bullet from a Gun". If it carried on much longer I thought I'd have to "Leave in Silence".' In fact the Israeli academic was by now almost completely incoherent, pushed to the edge of sanity by the revelations he had uncovered, only able to communicate using the titles of Depeche Mode songs. At the time of writing he sits in a secure room in the Menachem Begin Memorial Hospital in Tel Aviv repeating the words 'People are People' over and over again to himself. No one can get through to him.

Buckminster Powell is no nearer to answering the question of who or what is behind the information contained within the Code. Depeche Mode themselves deny any knowledge of the findings. Powell himself speculates that the Essex code may prove not only that God exists but that he is a fan of eighties music. That must bring little comfort to the family and friends of Ritz Krakas. It is doubtful that they 'Enjoy the Silence' in his now empty office.

FILE 7
THE WIVENHOE TRIANGLE

Just mention the Wivenhoe Triangle to a resident of Essex and they will shiver and shake like the eponymous ghost and elephant in the IPC comic of the early 1970s. It has been the subject of countless books, television documentaries, a pantomime with Geoff Capes and Gladiator Jet as Idle Jack, and even a popular motion picture The Wivenhoe Experiment starring Richard Widmark, Red Buttons and Gareth Hunt.

The Wivenhoe triangle.

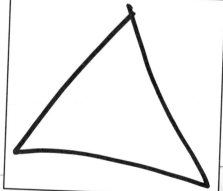

he Triangle – an isosceles – is formed by an imaginary line connecting the town with Tollesbury and Holland-on-Sea. The area within seems unremarkable, and indeed it is, for more than a hundred years nothing has happened. Absolutely nothing at all. Many people are convinced that this mysterious vacuum of activity is caused by a phenomenon unknown to science.

Nowt

Jolly Widescreen, author of two best-sellers about the region – *Vacuum in Wivenhoe* and *The Day of the Nothing* – has written:

> '*Despite the best efforts of local people to generate any kind of unusual activity such incidents stubbornly refuse to occur. Not only are events such as Strange Disappearances, Eerie Coincidences and UFO sightings completely unheard of but so too are more mundane, but noteworthy, happenings. No one ever receives an unexpected letter, or bumps into an old friend, finds a fiver balled up in a pair of old jeans, or gets three numbers in the lottery.*'

In fact, so stultiyingly ordinary is life within the Wivenhoe Triangle that many residents have made desperate attempts to create incidents that might bring a little sparkle to their otherwise staid and joyless lives.

X In 1945 Winston Churchill undertook a victory tour of the United Kingdom. Everywhere he went cheering crowds thronged the streets celebrating the Allied victory over the Axis powers. The Mayor of St Osyth was happy to welcome the entourage to his town. Sadly the Prime Minister's car broke down and the celebrations were abandoned.

Like everyone else Winston Churchill avoided Wivenhoe.

✗ In 1951 a mini Festival of Britain was organised in Brightlingsea. A modest-sized replica of the Royal Festival Hall was built out of Meccano including a two-thirds model of the Skylon. Although the event passed off without mishap it was generally perceived to be a failure, not lingering in anyone's memory for very long.

✗ In 1970 a local entrepreneur Davis Childes organised a massive two-day free rock festival. Despite a line-up which included Jimi Hendrix, the Rolling Stones, Donovan and Don McClean and the Crackerjack All Starz only twenty-three tickets were disposed of and the event was cancelled.

Zero

Wivenhoe has had a dull reputation since it was built by Richard De Muttely in the tenth century. Despite its agreeable climate, loamy soil and pleasant locale the area was shunned, regarded with strange indifference by conquering Normans and prosperous Elizabethans alike. Shakespeare in his early play *The Tragedie of the Alsatian Prince* referred to the town as Wivenhoe – a fact in itself unremarkable, for that was its name. The place was untouched even by Black Death in 1666, when the bubonic bacillus was accidentally trans-ferred *out* of the village in a bundle of cloth.

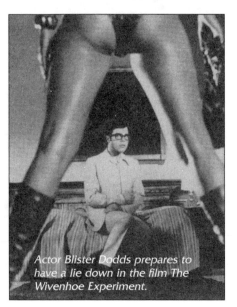

Actor Blister Dodds prepares to have a lie down in the film The Wivenhoe Experiment.

Bugger All?

For a very dull place the theories surrounding the Wivenhoe triangle are exotic to say the least. Author Jolly Widescreen explains his belief: 'The triangle covers the last remnant of the lost continent of Atlantis which is hidden beneath the soil. Many people think that Atlantis was the home of a race of techno-

Local writer Jolly Widescreen "it couldn't happen here"

logical superbeings who attempted to stabilise their volatile homeland by inventing a giant calming ray. The theory states that this ray is still operating today spreading its benign but bland influence over the entire area.'

Bubbly TV chef Ainsley Harriott has made a special study of the triangle and concludes: 'A race of alien mathematicians have been drawing huge triangles on our earth – or Sol 3 as they know it – for donkey's years. These form an electrical field which acts on the brainwaves of those within it. In Africa there's a huge hypotenuse that covers the whole of Zaire. The

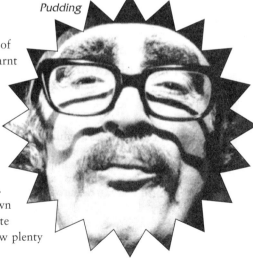

Rice: Pudding

square on its hypotenuse equals the sum of the square on its other two sides. I learnt that at school. Its the only time I've ever used it.'

Professor of Physics at Wivenhoe Metropolitan University, Rocketeer Kominsky has an even more outlandish idea involving towelling dressing-gowns, gravestones, ice, meningitis and the late Notorious B.I.G., but refuses to elaborate.

Arch-sceptic Larry Rice has his own theory: 'You'd have to be a complete pudding to swallow such nonsense. I know plenty of places like that. It's a load of shite.'

FILE 8
THE CHINGFORD FAERIES

Very special girls – Alice and Maud Peladon

O n a bright summer morning in June 1924, sisters Alice and Maud Peladon skipped out of their house, hand in hand towards the beautiful, bluebell-covered meadow that lay nearby. Devoted to each other, the girls would often spend their idle hours thus, making daisy chains, having dolls' tea parties and chatting with imaginary friends. The fact that Alice was thirty-three and Maud thirty-eight did not seem to concern them but in the words of local physician Doctor Edward Chops they were 'loonies'. However, for these very special girls that morning was to prove perhaps it was the world that was mad, not them.

Big Mental Girls

Maud had been playing with her spinning-top which whirled unexpectedly out of control and fell into a stream.

One of Alice and Maud's faerie cottages where they were witness to strange events.

Sir Linford Rillington-Place seen here in 1927, shortly before his arrest.

Attempting to retrieve it the girls became mesmerised by the sparkling water. They hitched up their summer frocks and set off downstream in pursuit of the bobbing toy.

After a while they found themselves deep in overgrown woodland and there made the extraordinary discovery that was to astonish the county.

Wading out of the water, the girls espied an enchanting collection of small wooden buildings. They realised at once that they had stumbled upon a faery dell. Excited but a little afraid they returned to their house to retrieve their little Box Brownie camera which had been a present from their beloved guardian – parish council leader Reverend Alec Aggedor.

Dell Boys

Upon their return the girls hid themselves with their camera and awaited the faeries' appearance. Many of the little houses showed signs of recent repair to their ramshackle structure, obviously the work of elfin hands. The girls saw through the window that each contained an old faery mattress, dirty faery blankets and a faery lamp. There were clear signs that the little people had been there recently including faery cigarette ends, and small jars of faery petroleum jelly.

Alice and Maud didn't have to wait long for a manifestation and they began snapping away, taking the first of the photographs that were soon to enchant all of Essex.

The girls couldn't wait to return home and tell Reverend Aggedor about their discovery. They explained how some of the figures they observed wore diaphanous clothes and had long flowing hair. They added that although some of them 'looked like ladies' they had the 'voices of men'.

The blurred images somehow found their way to local magazine *The Chingford Lady* which printed them and an interview with the girls:

Q. What exactly did you two young ladies see that day?
A. We went in woods. It was nice. We walked in stream.
Q. And what happened then?
A. The faeries come. There was older ones and younger ones. Some was big. Some was small. Hahahahahah.

Tiny detective Simon Buns seen here in an illustration from The Adventure of the Fancy Hats

Q. Calm down. What happened next?

A. They spoke in faery talk.

Q. What did they say?

A. Can't remember. The older one say something like 'come on, do it now' and the younger one took off his faery pantaloons.

Q. And what did you see then?

A. A magic wand.

Naturally there was opposition to the girls' story. Those trying to ascertain the whereabouts of the dell were not helped by Alice's somewhat vague description that it was 'in a place with grass and trees'. But Reverend Aggedor stood firmly, even vociferously, by his charges' version of events, eager to preserve 'the purity and innocence of their vision'.

A group of idle young men gather near a scout camp in Chingford. Nice Ian is first on the right.

Nice Buns

Inevitably the national papers picked up the story, chief among them The *Daily Sketch* which became a forum for an increasingly heated debate between noted author and spiritualist Sir Linford Rillington-Place – creator of world-famous detective Simon Buns – and leading sceptic the Bishop of Wrigley, Marcel McManus. Rillington-Place maintained that the blurred images without doubt showed 'ectoplasmic manifestations of ancient earth-spirits which originated in a realm other than our own'. McManus countered that the photos depicted nothing other than 'a load of whoopsies up to no good in a hut'.

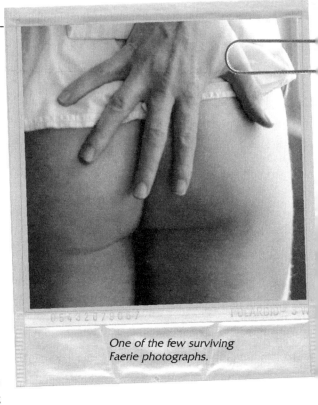

One of the few surviving Faerie photographs.

Certainly McManus's case was strengthened when Chingford police arrested a local petty thief called 'Nice Ian' already known to them for several acts of gross indecency. He alleged that the faery dell photographed by the girls was in fact disused gamekeepers' huts – a favoured haunt of 'local men who liked to go with other fellas'.

The girls themselves remained unaffected by all this controversy, having forgotten about it all within a month. They died in relative obscurity although 1967 saw a retrospective of their photographs when they shared an exhibition with Diane Arbus in New York. Reverend Aggedor, however, stuck firmly to his supernatural explanation of events until he died in 1947. 'But then he would have done,' said Nice Ian some years later. 'He was in half the pictures.'

FILE 9

MEAT UP IN THE SKY – THE STANSTED INCIDENT

Unidentified Flying Objects are now so much part of our lives these days that it feels as though they have always been with us. But not many people are aware that the phenomenon began in Essex one fine summer's day in 1947.

Balloon modeller and pilot Ricou Arnold.

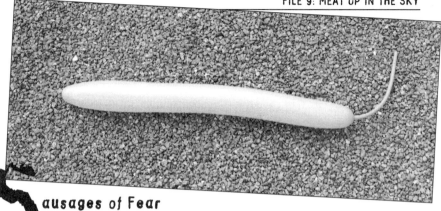

Sausages of Fear

Local pilot and balloon modeller Ricou Arnold took off from Rochford airfield near Southend heading for the Scottish borders where he hoped to pick up a consignment of tax-free rubber. 'I made my own balloons in those days,' he explained. As he soared over the mountain peaks something happened that changed his life for ever and sparked off the world's love affair with alien visitors.

Ricou Arnold's balloon model of one of the flying sausages that buzzed his plane.

'I was approaching the border when I saw a formation of very strange aircraft. They were long and cylindrical, with a mottled surface, pinky-white in colour. They were moving so fast I could hardly keep up with them. "My God," I thought, "they look like sausages, flying sausages"'

Arnold radioed home but his garbled communiqué about 'flying sausages' was misheard as *saucers* – leading to the popular misnomer that remains in use to this day. The frequency of sightings of saucer-like craft has tended to obscure the overwhelming number of encounters similar to Arnold's that have taken place in the Essex area.

Catalogue of Celestial Comestibles

X Lollipop man Jim Limes was ushering a group of children across the road when he was buzzed by a group of cylindrical pale brown soft-looking objects. 'If I didn't know better, I'd say it looked like a swarm of chipolatas,' he commented at the time.

Promoting the movie *A Hard Day's Night* legendary pop heroes the Beatles had a strange experience whilst driving through Dagenham. In an interview with Michael Parkinson in 1975 John Lennon recalled 'We was in the back of the limo when Paul said "Here lads, what's that noise?" It was a kind of sizzling sound. Ringo looked up and said "It's a pan." And we all looked out and saw this great big black shape with a protuberance like an enormous frying-pan. George was so scared that he tried to get out of the moving limo. At that point "the pan" rotated 180 degrees in our favour, revealing what I can only describe as a bloody great sausage.' The experience led Lennon to compose a song about the incident called 'Sausage to Fry' later retitled 'Ticket to Ride'. Speaking today from the Mull of Kintyre, Sir Paul McCartney says: 'The world was not yet prepared for what we saw, so I had John tone the whole thing down. I tell you, it put me off meat for life. The truth is, that's why I married Linda.'

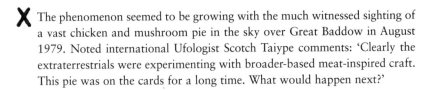 The phenomenon seemed to be growing with the much witnessed sighting of a vast chicken and mushroom pie in the sky over Great Baddow in August 1979. Noted international Ufologist Scotch Taiype comments: 'Clearly the extraterrestrials were experimenting with broader-based meat-inspired craft. This pie was on the cards for a long time. What would happen next?'

What indeed. Taiype's question was soon to be answered, in Spades.

Incident at Level 42

Spades, a small village outside Stansted airport was an unremarkable place – or at least it was until the night of August 5th, 1981 when residents were plagued by strange lights in the sky. They woke the following morning to find much of their village covered in a strange reddy-brown residue. Immediately alerted, Scotch Taiype made his way to the scene. Once there he took samples of the residue. 'There was no doubt about it. It was mince.'

A similar stringy mince-like substance had been found at the scene of other sightings. Scotch Taiype was convinced that this latest manifestation was merely the precursor to a much bigger incident. Sure enough four years later came reports that a mystery object had crash landed in a restricted area of Stansted

*Wing Commander
Tetanus Fermat –
"Giblets"*

*Scotch Taiype –
"expecting pies"*

Airport known only as Level 42. Taiype takes up the story: 'The airport authorities were already cordoning the place by the time I got there, but it was clear something strange was going on. There was gravy everywhere.' Taiype was forced to leave the area but he was determined to piece together the facts for himself. Years of research finally led him to retired Wing Commander Tetanus Fermat who had been in charge of the restricted area at the time. Fermat indeed had a strange story to tell. 'It was the one about the three billy-goats gruff and the troll under the bridge. When he finished he began talking about what exactly had taken place at Level 42.'

What exactly had taken place at Level 42

Fermat revealed that:

X A huge craft, which to human eyes resembled a stuffed chicken, made an abortive attempt to land on one of the runways at Stansted Airport, despite the fact there was an air traffic controllers strike on.

X The craft had burst upon impact scattering strange alien giblets over a large area. Witnesses reported a strong smell of sage and onion.

Is this a Chicken craft?

✗ Later that night a local butcher – Finlay Roundel – was called in and asked to bring 'three very big freezer bags' to the airport.

✗ A mysterious pliable metal of unknown origin but resembling tin-foil was wrapped around portions of the craft.

Fermat confirmed that a top-level D-notice was slapped on the whole affair by the Ministry of Defence. Fermat confesses: 'We put the story about that it was a failed experiment in giant in-flight catering – the idea being that you could save money by producing one enormous chicken to feed several plane-loads of passengers. To support this fantasy we even produced vast, impossible-to-open pats of butter in plastic containers.'

Despite this disinformation some civilians remained convinced that something mysterious had occurred, none more so than Finlay Roundel.

The Butcher

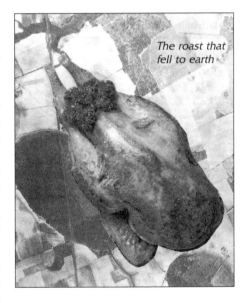

The roast that fell to earth

According to the butcher who supplied freezer bags to the base, an awesome sight awaited him when he arrived. 'In a hanger the size of...say...a large cash and carry was this...chicken. It was all cooked, nice and proper, you know...basted, but it was huge, like four grade-five Dewhurst outlets piled on top of each other. It had burst and all its giblets were spread around. I saw a liver as big as a chest freezer.'

Finlay Roundel was asked to open his enormous freezer bags and prepare his knives. 'This brass hat comes up to me and asks me to start carving it up. I've seen some joints of meat in my time but this just took the brisket.'

Photo revealing a giant hamburger supposedly sighted over Ilford

The Baker

After the chicken-craft was carved up, the freezer bags were rushed to a morgue where a strange autopsy was initiated. A controversial film record of this incident apparently survived. Unexpectedly this film resurfaced in Presstud Baker's Carlton documentary *Meat Up in the Sky*.

Although grainy, black and white and hand held, the footage does seem to show a very large parson's nose being removed from a bag and being dissected by a team of top men. A broad silver cabinet at one side resembles a hostess trolley and onto this the slivers of alien meat are carefully laid. At one point an argument appears to break out between the men about who was doing the carving with the result that one bursts into tears and the other storms out in a huff.

The Candlestickmaker

Doubts about the authenticity of the film however exist, particularly because of the Spice Girls calendar on the wall and Wispaccino wrapper visible in ashtray – a sweet not available until 1997, twelve years after the film was supposed to have been shot.

This possible forgery has tended to obscure a very real incident which may prove beyond doubt that sentient meat may lie beyond the farthest reaches of our solar system. Sadly there is no concrete evidence existing today, as Tetanus Fermat ruefully explained, 'An army marches on its stomach and the air force is no different. After we'd put the giblets in the freezer bags we cooked them and ate them. They were nice.'

This incident begs many questions. Were the meaty aliens alone in their interest in our little blue green world? Or, across the vastness of space, were there minds immeasurably superior to ours who watch this earth with envious eyes...

der...der...deeeeerrr

...and who slowly and surely draw their plans against us...?

de...de...de...der...der...wah...wah...wah...wah...wah...waaaah...der...der...der...
der...deeeeerrr...

FILE 10

TIGHTS OF POWER – NASTIDAMPNESS: ESSEX'S GREATEST PROPHET

Perhaps one of the most remarkable aspects of Essex's mysterious heritage is its record of astonishing predictions. It is as if the county acts as a locus for those blessed with the gift of prophecy or 'second sight'.

A rare woodcut of Nastidampness – note the staining around his crotch.

Over the years many personalities have earned the mantle of Prime Seer of Essex including Adam Weights, the so-called 'daft man of Thaxted'; Ginger Cuffs, whose amazing predictions included anticpating the invention of Sellotape; Lancaster Day-Oh, burnt alive for his heretical visions of the horrendous future of Basildon, now proved uncannily accurate, and of course seventeenth-century wise-woman Mammy Pamflett.

But perhaps the most extraordinary member of this exclusive club of seers was Renaissance enigma Nastidampness.

Sellotape – as predicted by Ginger Cuffs

A Small Prophet

Most controversial of all those who claim dominion in the strange world of predictions, the alchemist and advisor to the Crown known as Nastidampness was actually born Ralph de Gaunt in Billericay.

As a young boy Ralph developed an interest in gardening and this might well have been his chosen career had not an unfortunate medical condition intervened. This was to give rise not only to his strange nickname but also to his eventual expulsion from the houshold after one wet patch too many formed in the front of his tights.

Ralph's mother, a religious zealot who lived her life strictly according to the first five lines of the Old Testament was inspired by the story of Moses being left in the bull rushes and

Mammy Pamflett

Some Wee Predictions

Today experts agree that Nastidampness's predictions included:

✗ The rise to power and eventual fall of Adolf Hitler including details of the colour of his handkerchiefs and the size of his moustache.

Freddie Starr

✗ The development of air travel together with the provision for passengers of complementary white wine and non-dairy creamer.

✗ The invention of wireless telegraphy, television, and video games such as Pong, Galaxian and Space Invaders.

✗ The discovery of penicillin as well as recreational drugs such as White Doves, Rhubarb and Custards and Special K.

✗ The destruction of London either by flood or by a plague of angry cats.

decided to dispose of her embarrassing son in a similar fashion, despite the fact he was nearly fourteen years old.

Wrapping him in swaddling clothes, she placed him in a narrow air-tight box, or coffin, weighed him down with rocks and buried him in the churchyard. Wet with fear, Ralph waited for the end. Luckily, however, a kindly sexton, Hugh Shelves, saved the boy who would grow up to predict every major event of the twentieth century from perishing in a flood of his own making.

The Dirty Duke

Having unearthed Ralph, the sexton decided to take the young man under his wing. Several hours later, young Ralph emerged, shaken but wiser to the ways of the world. Taken in by the confirmed bachelor Shelves, Ralph was trained in the ways of the dibbler and the hose and also learned something about gardening. He eventually took up a post as chief groundsman to the superstitious Duke of Blackwater.

The dirty Duke of Blackwater

The Duke, an unpopular figure shunned by his peers, not only for his arcane beliefs, but for his undisguised obsession with other people's soiled underwear, took in young Ralph and encouraged him to cultivate a herb garden. It seems that it was whilst engaged in his botanical studies that Ralph's incredible visions began to emerge and he set them down in verse form. Ralph was already humiliated by his nickname Nastidampness so to shield himself from further ridicule he decided to disguise his predictions using a byzantine system of ciphers and metaphors.

As well as being interested in the condition of Nastidampness's tights, the Duke of Blackwater was convinced his employee could see into the future. Determined to profit by this he began circulating tracts of Nastidampness's work to the world at large.

The Quatrain now Arriving

Take this example from 1548:

> *'I look me there towards the West,*
> *My Oak and ash I like me best*
> *The rose and Bluebell round me thrive*
> *O, for their beauty, I'd gladly die.'*

Although at first glance these few lines seem fairly innocuous, they do in fact conceal a detailed prediction of the outcome of World War 2.

'I' means the Great War or World War I.

'Look' – The L in such close proximity to the I could suggest the Roman numerals for II i.e. World War II.

'me there' – Nastidampness tells us he is projecting his mind forward into the future.

'the West' – a reference to Fred and Rose West, the infamous Gloucestershire murderers. Rose is a conflation of Rosamund meaning 'Rose of the World'. Nastidampness is telling us that this terrible war will blight the whole globe.

'My Oak' – the symbol of Old England and all her brave allies.

'And Ash' – a clear allusion to Germany. The pop group Ash had a chart hit with the song 'Goldfinger', also the name of the third James Bond film. In this the central villain was played by Gert Frobe, a *German* actor.

'I like' – a contraction of 'I like Ike', the election slogan of legendary World War II General Eisenhower.

'me Best' – without doubt this refers to the footballer George Best who played for Manchester United, often the *winning* side.

It can be seen then how analysis of just the first two lines of this quatrain yields a devastatingly precise and unambiguous account of the latter stages of the last war.

Duke of Hazard

By the middle of the sixteenth century, under the Duke's patronage Nastidampness became a household word although admittedly a household word only used to describe areas of rotten plaster. And whilst the man himself modestly tended his gardens, the Duke saw fit to interpret his every word in order to bring his predictions to an eager paying audience.

One of these, stating that a massive earthquake, with its epicentre in Witham would destroy the entire eastern seaboard of England caused consternation amongst the superstitious population. The quatrain which apparantly contained this information:

'I like pansies, I like peas,
I like ants and bumble-bees'

President Dwight D. Eisenhower –
World War 2 victory predicted.

was said by some cynics to be just a stupid little poem about nature. However, the Duke insisted that the cataclysm would take place on Christmas Eve, 1552. When this failed to occur, Nastidampness's reputation went into something of a decline, although he continued to garden and to write his mysterious verse.

Sadly he did not foresee the Duke's own death (a freak accident saw him smothered in a pile of his protégé's unwashed hose) but freed from the Duke's interpretations the integrity of the prophet's original visions remains unimpaired to this day. Indeed its influence continued into the late twentieth century, when the structure of his system of impenetrable metaphor and stupid codes were used as a model for Dusty Bin's questions on the popular YTV game show *3-2-1*.

FILE 11

THE STRANGE CASE OF THE ESSEX GIRL JOKE

Anyone who was around in the mid to late 1980s will naturally remember a curious phenomenon that amused and titillated the whole country. It seemed trivial at the time but, as will be seen, of all the mysteries contained within this book, few are more extraordinary than the case of the Essex Girl Joke.

Q. *What does an Essex Girl use for protection during sex?*

A. *A bus shelter.*

oker

Q. What's the difference between an Essex Girl and a walrus?
A. One is wet, has a moustache and smells of fish – the other is a walrus.

Q. Why do Essex Girls use tampons?
A. So their crabs can go bungee jumping.

The chances are that these two jokes are familiar to you. A few years ago they and other examples of their kind were everywhere – the bar-room equivalent of Rubik's Cubes, the office version of Magic Eye pictures.* These jokes were specific to their time, part of our popular culture expressing contemporary concerns in humorous form. The fact that they have slipped in popularity in

---

* Except unlike Magic Eye pictures you didn't have to stand in front of them for half an hour and pretend you got them when in fact you didn't have a clue what they were. Nor as a phenomenon did Essex Girl Jokes first begin in the Athena shop windows with little groups of secretaries and shop workers standing around in front of them every lunchtime, before going on to appear in the collections of those men who sit on the pavements in town centres selling posters – usually a mixture of scratchy pictures of Bob Marley, giant paintings of cannabis leaves, or poor drawings of John Travolta with a misquoted line from *Pulp Fiction* – finally graduating to book form, rapidly descending from the plainly-titled 1, 2 and 3 to more lurid anthologies called things like the 'Magic Eye Karma Sutra' as the sales got smaller and smaller and publishing companies realised they had overcommitted to something that anybody could have told them in advance was going to be nothing more than a short-lived fad rather than a lasting and valid new medium. And unlike Rubik's Cubes they didn't first appear unheralded with one of the clever boys at school sat in the corner unnoticed, twisting it slowly, utterly absorbed in it. Nor was there a feeling, like there was with the Cube, that it was in fact insoluble once muddled up, and then Phil Clarkson came in one morning saying he'd done it but close examination in fact revealed that he'd just taken off all the stickers of a muddled one and put them back in the right order, but then somebody's older brother had worked it out and explained the formula to him and the challenge became how quickly you could solve it not whether you could solve it at all, and the flash boys like Richard Cohen and Digby Fryer whose dads were builders or bar-owners started turning it into a racket, putting bets on who could do it fastest until everybody lost interest. They were little cunts those kids. Swanning around like they were fucking royalty because they lived in big houses and all the girls fancied them. And the one time you did get invited to one of their parties your mum turned up too early to come and get you and came in and shamed you because everyone else made their own way home, they didn't have their mum come and pick them up.

recent years only confirms this, demonstrating how quickly our magpie minds move on to other things.

Brother Phil jealously guarding the world's first dirty joke book.

Penguin

To begin at the beginning, the first stirrings of this strange case can be found as far back as the fifteenth century in the fragile palimpsests of Brother Phil, a monk who wrote the world's first dirty joke book. Still to be seen in the archives of Southend Cathedral, the beautifully illuminated manuscripts contain much that is rare and ancient, including a joke about a man and a penguin, the entire first series of *Punt and Dennis* and this tantalising fragment:

> *Ponderable: What difference be there, 'tween a maid of Essex and a syllabub?*

> *Response: It costeth tuppence to lick out a syllabub.*

Clearly the womenfolk of the county were already developing a reputation for sexual looseness as well as empty headedness. In the 1930s, this example began to appear.

Q. What do you call an Essex Girl with an IQ of 150?

A. Basildon.

Riddler

However, it wasn't until the Conservative Party came to power in 1979, ushering in an era of unprecedented crassness, that the craze began to spread. Viewers of the last ever edition of *Parkinson* were shocked when the crumpled yet loveable interviewer ended his show with this riddle:

> **Q.** What does an Essex Girl do with her cunt after sex?
> **A.** She takes him down the pub.

Egghead

Soon the phenomenon was spreading like wildfire, faster, indeed than the Black Death of 1347. Clever-clogs historian Ingmar Sheets explains:

> *'The Black Death was carried by rats or, more properly, by their fleas, spreading from port to port across mainland Europe and making people's limbs and organs turn to a mass of suppurating gore. But the Essex Girl Joke was much faster. It could originate in a pub and be around the whole of England almost overnight.'*

Puzzler

Indeed the power of the joke was demonstrated in August 1991 when reformist Soviet President Mikhail Gorbachev, vacationing in his dacha on the Black Sea, was the victim of a putsch by hard-liners. Within twenty-four hours, somehow a new joke had appeared.

> **Q.** What do an Essex girl and President Gorbachev have in common?
> **A.** They both get fucked by eight men while on holiday.

King Tut

By now, Essex residents were concerned that the reputation of their beloved county was becoming tarnished. Local historian Dr Predator King of Tollesbury Metropolitan University set out to get to the root of the problem. 'I began by talking to people. That seemed to help as I'd spent the first few years communicating in a series of clicks and whistles, like a dolphin, and no one seemed to understand. No, the language thing was a definite breakthrough. Then, once people were talking, I'd write down what they said. That way I wouldn't forget before I got the bus home.'

Predator King – rude research

Bookworm

Having established the method of his research, Dr King had a strange experience. As he sat in his car one golden afternoon, looking out over Tollesbury, he glanced at his notes and had a shocking epiphany. He had been collecting data about the sexual activity of girls in the town and now he saw that the places where their congress had taken place were all connected, by invisible, arrow-straight lines.

Cemetery

'A girl called Jackie Catwoman told me she often went with boys in a bus shelter in Mr Freeze Street. I didn't believe her at first because she had a reputation as a bit of a Two-Face but in fact, it seemed quite a popular place for many young ladies to visit.

What was extraordinary was that it seemed to be directly linked to a local cemetery covered in poison-ivy which was equally popular, and you could draw a straight line to the towpath of the canal where thirty-eight women, all called Carol, told me they would do it for a Pernod and black.'

Excited by his discovery, King christened the phenomenon 'lay-lines' after the serial rutting which took place. But what connection could this have to the jokes still sweeping the country?

Lex Luthor

Here our primary source Laptop Carey comes up with the goods once more. His papers reveal that he'd made contact with palaeogeographer and stock-car champion Dixie Quatermass who had his own extraordinary theory. In his 1995 paper 'Essex: Pariah of Albion' he wrote:

Dixie Quatermass

'My special field of study is the formation of ancient landmasses, the enormous movements and stresses which shape the world we know. Continental drift, as outlined by Alfred Wegener, shows that the landmasses have moved about considerably since our planet was formed. There was once a land-bridge between Europe and Asia as well as a super continent which we call Pangaea. There was even a time when what we now call America was shaped like the pop-a-matic board-game Frustration, *but not for very long.'*

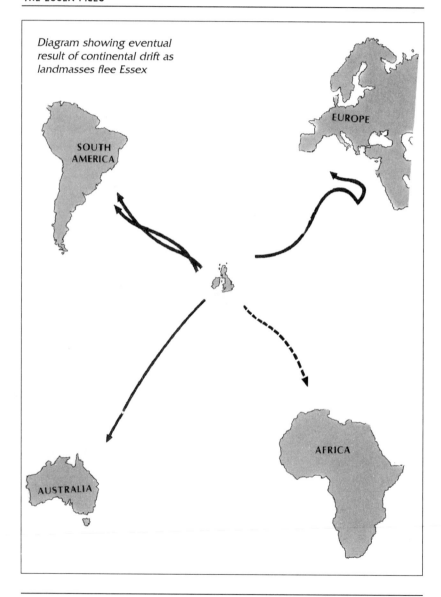

Diagram showing eventual result of continental drift as landmasses flee Essex

Brainiac

Years of research by Quatermass uncovered a secret document prepared by Alfred Wegener, the 'father of continental drift'. This showed that, throughout time, all the other landmasses had been attempting to *move away* from what we now call Essex.

'It was astonishing. It was like the continents had a grudge against the place,' commented Quatermass. Wegener had worked out that, at one time, Essex was surrounded by a volcanic 'ring of fire', such were the tectonic pressures on it. And this 'territory' corresponds exactly with Dr Predator King's lay-lines. The boiling, lava-strewn barrier would have effectively isolated the place for millennia, allowing all kinds of strange phenomena to evolve there. Wegener was convinced that something about the place was strange, possibly evil and that even the rocks themselves could not escape it. Aware of the explosive potential of his discovery, he sealed his manuscript in a tiny box and hid it in a drawer.

'It's just an awful place, you see,' laments Quatermass today. 'And that's why things like the Essex Girl Jokes proved so astonishingly popular. It stems from an ancient, almost instinctive need to take the piss out of the county. Nowhere else has ever suffered like we do.'

*Alfred "Jack" Wegener
– King of Crusts*

FILE 12

WHAT LURKS IN THE LAKE? – THE MONSTER OF ABBERTON RESERVOIR

Chipping Ongar aside, there is nowhere in Essex as forbidding and gloomy as the shores of Abberton Reservoir, one of the oldest and most mysterious bodies of water in the county. Nearly 300 yards across and as much as fifteen feet deep you could fit the entire population of Colchester into its murky and peaty waters. (Indeed in 1976 the entire population of Colchester did submerge themselves into Lake Abberton at the behest of Norris and Ross McWhirter in an ill-advised stunt staged for the BBC's popular Record Breakers series. The resulting tragedy proved the only black mark on the otherwise spotless record of the late presenter Roy Castle.) But Abberton is perhaps more famous for its legendary, rarely seen denizen, Little Titch.

Those are many famous lake monsters from Nessie to her Canadian counterpart Ogopogo to Mr Lips, the shy yet terrifying inhabitant of Japan's Lake Ikeda. For many, though, Little Titch is still the most baffling of these subaquatic creatures.

Holy Water

To find the first recorded sighting we must go back many centuries – to 760AD in fact, when St Bobby of France first attempted to bring Christianity to the nascent county of Essex. It was a cool spring day, and the missionary was bathing his weary sandalled feet in the waters of the lake. Suddenly his attention was caught by a gentle rippling. St Bobby looked on in astonishment as a weird creature reared from the water. It had a long, long swan-like neck, three distinctive humps on its back and

Artist's impression of Japanese Lake Monster, Mr Lips

Little Titch takes St Bobby of France for a ride

four diamond-shaped fins or flippers projecting from the side of its leathery hide. Remembering the experience of his compatriot St Columba, who had crossed Loch Ness on its monster's back, Bobby invoked the name of God and ordered this creature to carry him over the chilly waves of the reservoir.

The monster, cowed by the invocation of the Lord's name, did as he was bidden. Unfortunately St Bobby drowned. He had made a fatal error. The monster, though obedient to the word of God, was only eleven inches long.

Plain Crisps

Indeed the monster's size has been the key to its elusiveness all these years. Although local legend often related stories of the reservoir's mysterious beast, it was many centuries before Little Titch was seen again.

In the summer of 1928, Mr and Mrs Rex Crisps, a plain and ordinary couple, were holidaying on the banks of Abberton Reservoir. The B1026 had recently opened around the east-side of the lake and the Crisps were motoring along enjoying the view across the water. Their famous sighting of Little Titch, however, was to come from an altogether different direction. Mrs Crisps ordered her husband to pull up sharply after hearing a tiny cry.

Mrs Rex Crisps after an argument with her husband about Little Titch.

Thinking they may have hit a puppy the concerned bride jumped from the car and looked around in anguish. Seeing nothing Mr Crisps insisted they drive on until, to his astonishment, he spotted a very small shape cowering beneath the offside mudguard. Described later as being 'like something you'd see in the Natural History Museum only much, much smaller', the creature was licking one of its flippers with a tiny forked tongue. Bending down to examine the monster more closely and perhaps wrap it up in a handkerchief, the Crisps were startled when Little Titch waddled off squeaking into the water. Excited by their remarkable encounter, Mrs Crisps was keen to immediately contact the newspapers but her husband told her not to bother as 'it was nowt'.

Kettle Chips

In 1934 interest in the monster was revived when the famous 'Vet's Photograph' was published in the *Braintree Times*. The picture, taken by local veterinary surgeon Anton Kettle was controversial even in its day with many claiming it resembled a close-up of a crooked finger poking out of some bathwater or even a chip

The notorious Vet's Photograph – monstrous lake creature or finger in a sink?

floating in a bowl. But whatever its authenticity, the photograph was responsible for spreading Little Titch's fame throughout the county.

Monster Munch

A rash of sightings in the early 1970s led the famous naturalist and TV weatherman Sir Jack Scott to suggest a full sonar sweep of the mysterious reservoir. After public disinterest scuppered these ambitious plans, Sir Jack resorted to swimming the length of Abberton with a snorkel and a Polaroid camera wrapped in cling-film. The resulting image convinced Sir Jack that a mysterious beast did indeed dwell in the peaty waters. It survived by feeding on a mixture of pizza boxes, used condoms and old prams. Categorising it scientifically as like 'a prehistoric plesiosaur, only dead little, obviously' he dubbed the creature *Abbertoneras Miniscules* – literally 'tiny Abberton Monster'. A few weeks later, some wag pointed out that if you rearranged the letters you could form the phrase 'the Abberton Reservoir monster is a gigantic hoax'! A few weeks after that some other wag pointed out that this was rubbish, and that the best you could get out of it was 'rubber man eats lici son'.

Whatever the implications of Scott's research there seems little doubt that another piece has been added to our Essex jigsaw of mystery – maybe not an edge bit, or a piece of the sky, but quite an important one anyway. We have little doubt that something dwells beneath the murky waters of Abberton. It's just very, very small.

FILE 13

THE MIRACLE OF PATSY PALMER

Unexplained holy visions have sanctified sites all over the world, attracting hundreds of thousands of pilgrims each year seeking solace, healing or merely an unusual holiday in the company of the severely disabled.

Juliette Mates poses as her heroine Bianca

Cum-Hole

Essex is not without its fair share of such shrines. Two nine-year-olds from Beaumont-cum-Hole were witness to an apparition in late 1953 of a 'brilliant lady in white' with tinsel for hair and a dress made of delicate net. Hundreds flocked to the children's house before the mysterious figure was revealed as nothing more than the fairy on top of the Christmas tree looked at through binoculars.

Burning Orb

Three twelve-year-old girls from Pitsea announced that they had seen 'the holy Family up in the sky' in an incident that came to be referred to as the 'Pitsea Visions'. The sighting took the form of a large burning orb that hung suspended amongst the clouds. Upon later investigation it turned out to be the sun.

But not all such occurrences have been so easily dismissed.

Juliette

The story begins with fifteen-year old Loughton schoolgirl Juliette Mates. 'She's always been a big *EastEnders* fan,' explains Juliette's mother

The Queen visiting the site of the Pitsea Visions

Wheaty, 'ever since the early days – mainly because like the troubled Watts family we had a poodle called Roly, though ours only had three legs. But it was when the character of Bianca was introduced that Bernie began watching every episode. I think it's because she's a ginger like Bianca.'

Soon after Bianca's first appearance Juliette was tuned in not only every Monday, Tuesday and Thursday but also to all eighty-five minutes of the Sunday omnibus too. Soon posters of actress Patsy Palmer covered her bedroom walls. Wheaty confesses: 'There's hell to pay if she misses an episode. I think it's her colouring. It makes her fiery and hot-headed, just like her on-screen counterpart.'

Romeo

Juliette began to notice something strange was happening around the time of Bianca's driving lessons with Albert Square Romeo, David Wicks – played by heart-throb gay-boy actor Michael French. 'It was a turbulent time for poor Bianca,' recalls Wheaty,

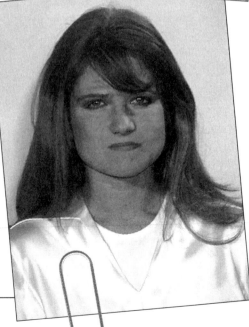

'there she was attracted to this hunky older man, all those hormones sloshing around. Then all of a sudden she finds out that he was her father. She was very upset.' Juliette was upset for her, but the teenager's distress turned to confusion when she next glanced at the poster on her wall.

'I'd always liked this picture 'cos Patsy's smiling this big smile in it,' the flame-haired teenager elucidates, 'but I was lying in bed and I looks up, yeah, and she looks really sad, innit. She's got this big frown on her forehead. I told dad the next day but he didn't believe me.'

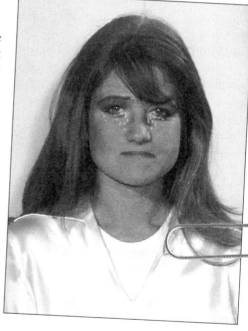

Victor

Dismissing his daughter's story as teenage fantasy Mr Victor Mates forgot all about the incident. It was only when Juliette's room began to be crowded with her schoolmates that he began to take notice. Victor Mates remembers the time well.

'Ricky was sleeping with Bianca's best friend Natalie. Naturally when poor Bianca found out she was heartbroken. And when large groups of Juliette's schoolfriends began sitting in her bedroom until two or three in the morning we knew something was up.'

Foxtrot

It transpired that the picture of actress Patsy Palmer had changed again. This time she wasn't just frowning. She was crying.

'It was amazing,' says Foxtrot Sticks, one of Juliette's schoolfriends, 'all of her make-up had run down her face. It had taken the foundation off and you could see the spots underneath.' Another girl recalls touching the picture around the cheeks and feeling wetness.

Foxtrot Sticks

Proud parents Wheaty and Victor Mates.

Persuaded that something truly magical had happened the girls established their own religion called Biancism. They are reluctant to reveal what the religion actually involves but Mrs Mates notes that they have all grown their hair long and had it dyed ginger. 'Some of them have drawn freckles on their faces with an eyebrow pencil and they all scowl a lot,' she observes.

The Miracle of East 17

Juliette has also reported that some of the other pictures on her wall seem to have been affected by Patsy Palmer's mysterious animation. A big fan of

Walthamstow tearaway boy-band sensation East 17, Juliette has had a poster of the group above her bed for nearly two years. When outspoken Brian Harvey was sacked over his ill-advised boasts about the amount of the lethal dance drug Ecstasy he had necked in one night, Juliette noted that his image vanished from the photograph. Recently it has reappeared just as unofficial group leader Tony Mortimer's has began to fade.

She also notes that a postcard of former Take That star Robbie Williams has 'put on an awful lot of weight' over the past few months.

Other Soap Shrines

Bizarre though this phenomenon may seem it is not confined to Juliette's bedroom. In 1989 Trent Beaker, a *Coronation Street* fan from Exeter, reported that the picture of Anne Kirkbride – who plays beleaguered widow Deirdre Rachid in the long-running soap began weeping real tears when her then-husband Ken left her for council worker Wendy Crozier. 'It's even stranger when you think that you never see Deirdre cry for real in the programme,' Mr Beaker commented, 'because Anne can't do tears.'

Rabbi Vivien Herring

In 1983 Rabbi Vivien Herring, a keen follower of the long-running twice-weekly children's drama serial *Grange Hill* reported seeing a vision of Erkan Mustapha who played the unpopular fat boy Roland. 'He was wearing a beret and complaining that Gripper had been calling him "Gutsy".'

FILE 14

FURRY FRIENDS – THE TIPTREE PANDA AND OTHER BEASTS

Over the years, we have become used to reading reports of unexplained accounts of wild animals roaming the idyllic English countryside. Tales of the famous Surrey Puma tearing the throat and insides from flocks of sheep, or the Wakefield Anaconda squeezing its victims to an early grave, are the common currency of tabloid centre-spreads. But to come face to face with such a phenomenon is another matter.

High Sierra

If he had been on safari in Kenya, the sight which greeted car mechanic Glen Deacon on the frosty morning of November 8th 1989 would have come as no surprise. But Glen was not on safari. He was fixing a new exhaust to a Ford Sierra in the little town of Tiptree and was not expecting anything out of the ordinary. Glen takes up the story:

'So there I was, lying underneath this jacked-up Y-reg Sierra. The holding bracket on this model is notorious for having too much give in it, meaning your silencer rattles around like a pea in a drum. There's one screw in particular where the thread always slips. But if you take the bracket system off an old Granada – any model between '78 and '85...no '86, and spot-weld it to the centre of the chassis...oh, sorry. You was asking about the beast. Well, yeah, I looked up and there was a panda standing there.'

A mysterious creature sighted in farmland near Tiptree proved to be an angry Cavalier King Charles Spaniel called Solomon.

Car Mechanic
Glenn Deacon

Panda Monium

For many years there had been rumours of a strange furry, two-tone beast rummaging in bins and swinging on climbing frames in recreation grounds and private gardens but until Mr Deacon's experience there had been no close encounter. Many theories had been advanced as to what this creature might have been ranging from a bizarre hybrid of domestic cat and bear, to a large, badly observed magpie.

With hindsight perhaps it should have been clear what genus this beast actually belonged to. Garden cane and bamboo kitchen blinds had been disappearing for a period of some months. But once identified, the panda's reign of terror seemed to escalate. Scores of local households were bothered, with reports of the creature, breaking into children's bedrooms and demanding affection. One family, the Andersons, stated:

> 'We were woken by a noise in the kitchen and came down to find an empty jar of Gale's honey, and sticky paw prints all over the lino. We crept through into the living-room and we couldn't believe our eyes. There was this bloody great panda rolling around on top of a beach ball wearing one of the kid's anoraks. When he saw us he seemed a bit scared but he opened his arms like he wanted a cuddle. We couldn't help but feel sorry for him.'

Koala Shaker

The mysterious panda was not the only wild beast to be spotted roaming freely across the Essex countryside, and in fact an incident at Stansted Airport served to deepen the enigma. Lufthansa pilot Ritter Sporte explains what happened:

> 'I was approaching the runway, preparing to land the plane. It's always a difficult manoeuvre, even with today's technology and the development of automatic piloting, it's the part that requires the most concentration. You have to keep one eye on the altimeter and the other on the

runway level threshold which is set by a computer – I don't know if you have seen the American picture Die Hard 2: Die Harder *with Bruce Willis and Bonnie Bedelia reprising her role as his hard-pressed wife, but in that movie the runway level threshold is raised artificially causing a terrible crash. It's fanciful but it's not far from the truth…oh sorry…ja, ja…you were asking about the animals…well I looked down and there were all these bloody koalas on the runway.'*

It transpired that a family of the loveable Australian creatures were making their way to the international departure lounge, in which stood the lone eucalyptus tree which had become their home. For many weeks flights were seriously delayed, because passengers refused to board without stroking and cooing over the adorable creatures.

Bush Whacked

These sightings of wild and fluffy animals were growing too numerous to ignore. By the end of 1991 a team of crack RSPCA officers had been called out to bring an end to this inexplicable menace. Armed with the latest in soft nets, nicely

RELATED SIGHTINGS

Low-flying dogs in Dagenham

Buffalos in Braintree

Chinchillas in Colchester

Long-eared lemmings in Leigh-on-sea

Strippy zebra on parcel shelf of white Ford Escort

padded cages and tempting chocolates the team moved into the areas of the county from which the reports had emanated.

The team faced their greatest challenge following the infamous bush-baby riots in the spring of that year. A colony of the incredibly cute animals had made their home in the eaves of Colchester Cathedral. When the officers moved in, equipment at the ready the public fought back shouting 'Leave them alone!', 'They've done you no harm!' and 'Oh, haven't they got lovely big eyes!' The resulting disturbance led to increasing pressure to find a solution to the mystery of where these creatures had come from.

The Theories

1. A wormhole in time and space with its event horizon in Africa and Australia has created a corridor between Essex and these exotic continents.

2. The creatures observed are in fact genetic mutations of domestic animals caused by sunspot activity distorting the replication of their DNA.

3. As a nation of animal lovers, the people of Essex are merely projecting the beasts from their own collective unconscious.

4. A mysterious alien force is somehow bringing life to inanimate cuddly toys.

5. A small private zoo in Bishop's Stortford run by businessman Ron Tandy closed down in October of 1989 and did not redistribute its animals as promised but released them into the wild.

Whichever one of these theories eventually proves correct, the people of Tiptree are not likely to forget the day the animals came.

*Do wild
beasts roam
Tiptree?*

Yes , , ,

. . . they do.

FILE 15

DID CHRIST DIE IN HATFIELD BROADOAK?

The town of Hatfield Broadoak is one of the more obscure areas of the county of Essex, famous, if at all, for its delicious current bun – Jessie's Wonder – and not a lot else. But, tucked away in an obscure corner of the town's oldest cemetery lies something which may just be the most important religious relic in the entire world. Behind the rows of shattered gravestones and weathered angels stands a plain, functional tomb bearing the legend:

'Edmund Joyce 1835–1870.
And God took him in his rest that he might succour him. Sadly missed by Eunice and the boys.'

Jessie's Wonder
– a bun.

Local

What would appear, at first sight, to be the innocuous resting place of an obscure Victorian gentleman is, in fact, something altogether more extraordinary. For, according to local legend, it is nothing less than the tomb of Jesus Christ.

This astonishing idea is upheld not only by the guardian of the tomb, council worker Robbie Trilobite, but by the followers of the 'Sect of Joyce's Wet Bones', a cult of some sixty members dedicated to spreading the truth about the Messiah's last repose. But how could Jesus have ended up in Essex some two thousand years after his supposed death? Leader of the sect, Alison Machines, takes up the story:

'After what we last hear of Him in the New Testament, the crucifixion, the resurrection, appearing to his chums and that, we believe that Jesus left Palestine on an extended walking holiday. I mean, he wouldn't have had very good memories of the place, would he? He probably needed a bit of time to himself.'

Modest

Machines assert that Jesus took rather more than a bit of time – almost two millennia – to 'get His shit together' and then made his way to England, where the climate was more agreeable. By now known as Edmund Joyce and earning a living as an itinerant salesman, the Messiah preached about love, peace, understanding, forgiveness and fancy goods until He ended up in Hatfield Broadoak. Here He rented a modest apartment, as befitted Him, paying a shilling a week for a box room at the top of a house belonging to a Mrs Violet Cott.

William Joyce was a model of propriety. He even wore a top hat whilst bathing.

Mrs Cott's house today.

But there are further shocks for those not expecting a 'second life of Christ'. According to Robbie Trilobite, also an adherent of the sect, Edmund 'Jesus' Joyce was persuaded to marry Mrs Cott's daughter Eunice. 'It's entirely in keeping with Him being the Son of Man,' argues Trilobite. 'Taking a bride would all be part of His plan and Mrs Cott must've known what a catch He was. Anyway, Eunice was three months up the stick.'

Contended

According to the Sect of Joyce's Wet Bones, the Messiah lived a happy and contented life, fathering six boys and opening a shop before succumbing to a brain-fever at the age of thirty-five, exactly the age Jesus Christ was said to be upon his death, if you add a couple of years.

The temptation to dismiss the whole story as a ludicrous fabrication is strong, but the legends about Edmund Joyce are numerous. He was known to go to church, particularly at the time of the big festivals. He was said to be particularly fond of the midnight mass on Christmas Eve because he 'loved a good sing-song'. He wore his brown hair quite long and, though he was clean-shaven, looked quite a bit like Robert Powell from ATV's *Jesus of Nazareth*. And he was good with his hands, often making furniture for Eunice and his children with the skills of a born carpenter.

Tinker

Someone who knew him vaguely was local dignitary Ivan Palladio, responsible for turning down Joyce's application to become a mason. Writing in his diary in September 1858, he said:

'Had that twat Joyce on at me again. The likelihood of him ever amounting to anything in this town is most unlikely. Fella's little more than a travelling tinker. Yet to hear him speak, you'd think he was Jesus Christ Almighty.'

Mrs Violet Cott
getting into a bath

Gone

Of course, Christian theology declares that the Messiah died on the cross and was then resurrected. But are we to interpret this as a spiritual rebirth or a physical one? In the New Testament, much is made of Christ's actual, physical resurrection. When Mary Magdalene and her friend Harry arrived at the tomb they found that the body had gone and the great stone that sealed it had rolled away. Harry blamed poor masonry, saying the tomb was jerry-built but Mary knew differently. Some time after this, He appeared to two hitch-hikers on the road to Emmaus and dined with them in a very unghostly fashion, saying that he was 'knackered' and that his wrists and feet were 'giving him gyp'.

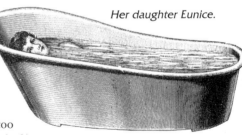

Her daughter Eunice.

Is

Finally, he appeared to His disciples who were 'really put out, as though they had seen a spirit' until Christ persuaded them he was flesh and blood by playing a game of five-a-side and telling rude jokes.

Bearing all this evidence in mind, is it too much to suppose that Jesus lay in some kind of coma after his crucifixion, got better and then left Palestine for a prolonged period? And is it also too much to suppose that the Lamb of God returned to us in another human guise, that of Edmund Joyce, Hatfield Broadoak merchant?

Yes it is.

FILE 16

THE CHEEKY MAN OF CHELMSFORD

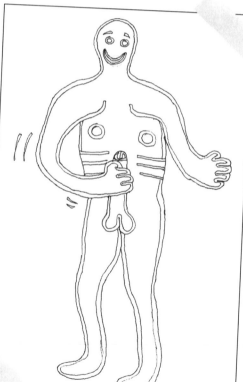

Standing proud – The Cheeky Man of Chelmsford.

The county of Essex has seen many oversized phenomena throughout its history: the world's biggest kebab – over one and a half miles in length – was barbecued in the village of Iclingham in 1973; Essex-born writer John Fowles once wrote a novel so long and fat that the height of the manuscript inspired the title of his next book *The Height of the Manuscript*; and the country's worst milk-slick hit Frinton-on-Sea in 1958 when a ferry from the Hook of Holland collided with an enormous shoal of angry sea-horses.

Mick the Bugger 'makinge lewd withe an passing womane'

But many people are not aware that the county itself was once used as a vast artist's canvas. For the chalky downs and grassy plains of the rolling Essex countryside are a testament to ancient man's primitive aesthetic sensibilities, the power of his imaginative vision and the sheer muckiness of his mind.

Big Hard Cock

Some 'hill figures', as they are known, date from fairly recent times. A gigantic white coat was cut into the chalk of the hills of Sible Hedingham in 1913. An anti-Suez protester cut a rude silhouette of prime minister Anthony Eden in a peat bog near Rayleigh and an eccentric ostler spent half his life tattooing the image of a tiny hill onto the side of his favourite white horse. But others have a more mysterious lineage, none more so the notorious Cheeky Man of Chelmsford. Etched into the living rock above the bustling market town is the stylised figure of a male, long of limb, with a face full of mischief and, in its clenched fist, a big hard cock the size of a double-decker bus. Two hundred feet long, the giant's body and astonishingly naughty tackle have a long and bewildering history, although the date of the drawing's execution remains obscure.

A History of Cheekiness

X The first record of the figure appears to be contained in the traditional Essex folk-song 'Giant John Barleycorn Went a Diddlin', the second verse of which begins: 'Sing ri-fo-lo, a diddle o a dee, ri-fo-lo o dale, John's got wood, John stands proud, John's got a stiffie like a coffin nail.'

X In 1360 the giant became the focus of the so-called 'Rude Riots', when local agitator Dag Nabbit and his followers rebelled against the Church's anti-fornication tracts by camping out on the figure and waggling their naked backsides at the spires of Chelmsford.

Agitator Dag Nabbit having a wee.

X The Cheeky Man is mentioned in the famous 'Tour of the Isles of Britain on a Pig' by diarist and scholar Dr Emmanuel Flesh. He described how folklore attested that any virginal girl who desired to become pregnant would do so if she sat on the end of the giant's proud member without her underwear. Flesh wryly observed that they 'could get up the duff much quicker if they'd sat on the bell end of mine'.

X Prudish Victorians did not take kindly to the giant and his oversized member. When the Queen herself visited Chelmsford in 1870 for the annual Festival of Coins frantic efforts were made to censor the offending figure. Engineers laboured tirelessly to shift enormous sheets of tarpaulin up the hillside. Unfortunately the operation ran out of funds and only three quarters of the figure was covered, everything in fact except the offending organ.

THE 1965 ARCHEOLOGICAL DIG

In 1965, a team of archeologists from the Ancient Filth Laboratories, led by Essex-based scientist Dr Jilly Pad, decided to excavate the area surrounding the giant. The revolutionary equipment they used on the Cheeky Man's equipment was designed to discover if the ground had been disturbed in the recent past. Their work uncovered remarkable results:

X Once, a whole series of huge, teardrop-shaped white depressions had once been visible, shooting out of the giant's penis. Although Dr Pad refused to elaborate on their exact meaning she did comment, 'Well, it's pretty bloody obvious, isn't it?'

X The hindquarters of what may be a cow had also once been carved in close proximity to the giant's loins, re-enforcing the theory that the figure represented sixteenth-century idiot 'Mick the Bugger'.

X The giant had once worn a big hat, but that wasn't very interesting.

*Dr Emmanuel Flesh
– "Bell End"*

The Queen however was unfazed, commenting 'Eeh, don't fret. It's nowt I've not seen before.'

X The Cheeky Man was still causing controversy in the supposedly permissive 1970s when the HTV teatime mystery serial *The Children of the Penis* was filmed on location in Chelmsford. Deemed 'far too dirty' for its 4.45 time slot, the finished product was shelved and replaced with repeats of *Follyfoot*.

Theories of Cheekiness

Although no one is sure exactly who or what the Cheeky Man represents there are a number of hypotheses:

✗ Local legend states that the giant is a satirical representation of sixteenth-century Chelmsford village idiot 'Mick the Bugger', famous for his cavortings with local farm beasts and his adventures in self-abuse.

✗ Another story tells of an enormous giant who strayed from nearby Ipswich suffering from terrible priapism – or a permanent erection. Seeking to cool his member in the spring-waters of Chelmsford he lay face down on the hillside and became stuck in a pothole. The local people killed him with sticks, turned him the right way round and then carved around his outline in the living chalk. This theory has since been disproved by science.

✗ A party of drunken druids returning from a mead festival cut the figure overnight in an act of naughty, drunken bravado.

Whatever the truth, the Cheeky Man retains his secret, a secret as enigmatic as the grin carved all over his big Neolithic face.

A rare still from the never broadcast TV series Children of the Penis

FILE 17
THE RAIN OF TERROR

The expression 'to rain cats and dogs' is used to describe an unusually heavy downpour. But, in the strange world we now know we live in, it can sometimes have a more specific meaning.

Collector of all things bizarre Charles Homer Abyss seen here with a colostomy bag found during a rain of surgical appliances.

Reports of strange rains are as old as History itself. There have been showers of frogs, fish and even horses. as shown in this cutting from *The Inverness Courier* of 1881.

'Much was made yesterday of a report by local widow Mrs Waterhouse Meal. The lady, approaching seventy-five years of age, stated that a loud whinnying sound in her garden was followed by the fall of over thirty horses from the sky. All landed on their legs and appeared to have suffered no ill-effects. Mrs Meal is contemplating opening a stud-farm.'

Other Phenomena

Other phenomena include showers of knickers, pasta, paperbacks, beer and, in one extraordinary case, over forty-two thousand tiny models of the *Cutty Sark*. But, as we might expect, the most consistent and bizarre occurrences have been in the county of Essex.

An incident is recorded in the ancient Book of Nells, an illuminated manuscript dating from the fourth century. Amongst the records of commonplace transactions and day-to-day life is this curiosity:

'A manne cum to thee Parish of Ingattestone, looking like as he Had had a greatte frite. Ask'd wahtte ail'd him he spake thatt an Quantity of breaded scampi hadd falled From th'Heavens and cover'd him from pate to toes. When we laffed like as the drainnes he took us outside and there we didde see the ground to be cover'd in the stuff. It was horrid.'

A rare illustration from the book of Nells showing a man riding a dog.

And this was no isolated incident. It seems that, unlike other areas afflicted by falls of fish, eels and whelks, Essex is uniquely hit by *ready-prepared* sea-food.

In 1649

In 1649 the country was agog over the recent execution of King Charles I. What would the new order bring wondered the frightened population of West Mersea? Well, rather to their surprise, while the rest of England got a republic, West Mersea got a monsoon of crabsticks. So prolonged and numerous were the showers, indeed, that a parliamentary force was completely wiped out by the viciously barbed morsels which speared their flesh 'like little javelins'. The fishy smell was said to be so overpowering that no strangers came near the town for almost two decades.

Other Strange

Other strange showers that are often reported take the form of coloured rain. Black rain, yellow rain and even blood have been seen but while rational theory points to desert dust becoming mixed up with the precipitation, this can hardly explain what happened in Canvey Island in the summer of 1958.

It was a blazing hot day and young Fiodor Dairy-Lea was taking an afternoon off from revising for his A levels. He had decided to go to the cinema and, afterwards emerged into the sunshine happy and contented.

'It was a cloudless day,' he recalls. 'I went to see the Hammer *Dracula* with my friend Alan. We

Well hung student and expert on flavourings Fiodor Dairy-Lea.

were very impressed. Christopher Lee was a far more persuasive Count than ever the pantomimic Lugosi had been. He brought a fantastic, animal sensuality to the role. Well, we got as far as the top of my road when a cloud appeared out of nowhere and blocked the sun. Me and Alan looked up and suddenly there was this stuff falling all over us. It should've been rain but it was far too thick. Kind of creamy with bits of gherkins in it.'

Looking closer, Fiodor, an expert on flavourings, recognised sugar, egg, spirit vinegar, capers, acetic acid, modified maize starch, salt, mustard, flavouring, stabiliser guar gum, and titanium dioxide. 'It was clear to me that we had been hit by a shower of tartare sauce,' he says in wonder.

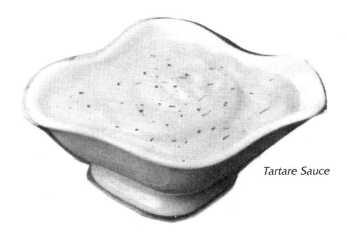

Tartare Sauce

The Legendary

The legendary collector of all things bizarre Charles Homer Abyss had his own very particular theories as the origins of the Essex falls. Throughout his life he published a variety of books including *There Are Things Up There*, *Watch it!*, *Stinks* and the best-selling *Heaven's Bracelets*. In each, he expanded upon his theories which we can present, for the first time, as a unified whole.

1. The falls are debris from collisions between giant interplanetary sea-food merchants whose strange craft ply the wastes of space between Venus and Mars.

OTHER FAMOUS MYSTERY RAIN CASES FROM ESSEX

A sample from the '87 vomit downpour at Basildon.

The only photograph of the infamous (and very fattening) 'M&M monsoon of Maldon'

A quick shower of knickers and bras at Saffron Walden is caught on camera.

2. Snacks from the pockets of vast space-giants have fallen to Earth whilst their owners were looking for their keys.

3. A heavenly river, what Charles Homer Abyss called the 'super Thames', runs around the planet and its denizens periodically fall to Earth. This fails to explain why all the falls have been treated and processed.

4. In ancient Greek legend, Zeus, king of the gods, was surrounded by his contemporaries, including Athena, goddess of posters and Mercury, the god of cheaper telecommunication. Whilst Zeus enjoyed his life, after several million years on Mount Olympus, he fancied a change. So he employed one of those little men who bother people in pubs to come up and sell him baskets of sea-food. This man, known as Ricky, did great service to the gods and, when he died, Zeus placed him amongst the stars as the constellation Crustaceus – the Prawn. According to Abyss, Zeus' cast-offs still somehow find their way to us through the rain.

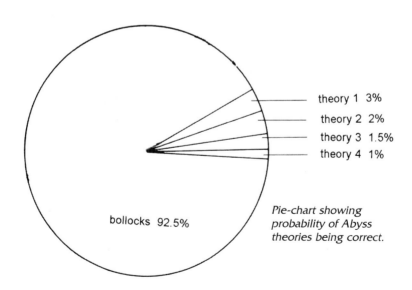

theory 1 3%
theory 2 2%
theory 3 1.5%
theory 4 1%

bollocks 92.5%

Pie-chart showing probability of Abyss theories being correct.

FILE 18
THE HARLOW NIGHTIE

At a quarter to ten one cold November morning in 1996 two ex-priests broke open a dirty old tea chest. It was no ordinary day for the former men of God, Father Terry Knight and the 'Reverend' Tommy Videos, for they were about to reveal to the world a most mysterious artefact.

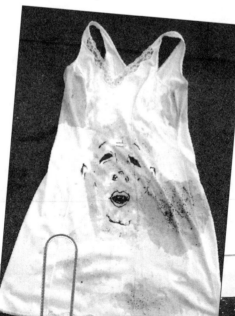

The Harlow Nightie – the most precious holy relic in all of Essex

nside the tea chest, wrapped in an old Fine Fare carrier bag was a fragile piece of material in the shape of a nightdress. The two men unrolled the item with shaking hands revealing mysterious yet distinctive markings suggestive of human occupation. This was nothing less than the garment worn by St Julie, the patron saint of low and vulgar women, in which she is said to have died in 1952: The Harlow Nightie.

Relics of Old

In olden days, churches often quarrelled about the amount and quality of the religious artefacts in their keeping. Bones and teeth and hair sprang up everywhere. In 1567, Biblical scholar Tomorrow Pipps was able to build a gazebo in his garden out of splinters said to come from Christ's cross. A nun on the Isle

Julie Saint hitching her stockings up.

of Sheppey lived inside a big hollow foot which once belonged to St Paul. And a walking, talking automaton rumoured to contain the last meal eaten by St Nicholas inside its wooden belly was exhibited at a fair in Rome in the early eighteenth century.

But, by the 1960s the practice of keeping such relics had become discredited. Only the Harlow Nightie was to retain its mystical significance.

Shoved in Bag

The unveiling of the nightie after forty years of controversy gave rise to renewed speculation. Had it really wrapped the body of St Julie of Harlow? Or was it, as some cynics suggested, just a mucky old bit of nylon, covered in stains and shoved in a plastic bag because someone forgot to take it to the launderette? Perhaps Science could provide an answer.

A Night to Remember?

St Julie was born plain Julie Saint in Harlow in 1912 on the day the *Titanic* went down (intriguingly she died in similar circumstances forty years later when a local wrestler called Titanic went down on her.).

There is little information about her early life except that she was known to be a forward girl who enjoyed the company of boys in return for a Woodbine or a penn'th of chips. Apprenticed in a hot-water bottle factory she drifted into a life of vice, supplementing her meagre factory wage with money earned from the touch of men.

Christ Almighty

Popular with the punters because of her energy and knockabout sense of humour, Julie took up residence opposite a

The Reverend Tommy Videos

Father Flanagan Knight – besotted with a common whore

Methodist chapel in Frontispiece Street and it was here that her unexpected canonisation was initiated. One of her regular clients was the chapel's minister, Father Flanagan Knight who would often regale his young son Terry with tales of Julie's remarkable gifts. 'He said she was an angel,' recalls Terry, 'sent from God to give men pleasure.' As a result of these endorsements word began to spread that Julie was a divine presence, a school of thought only confirmed by the cries of 'Jesus Christ! Oh Jesus Christ!' coming from her bedroom window late at night. Clearly Julie was seeing visions of Our Lord.

For many years Julie prospered, until her unfortunate final trick with the aptly named Titanic. After her death she was cremated in the chapel and at her request her ashes were collected in a Dutch cap and flushed down the toilet. Broken-hearted Flanagan Knight never recovered and died a little over a year later in 1953.

Secrets of the Slip

Terry Knight takes up the story:

'About ten years later I was taking holy orders myself – I was working as a waiter at a seminary – and I began to hear stories about a nightdress with mysterious properties. Just before he was defrocked, my father had canonised Julie and local people had come to regard her as a real saint. There was a lot of interest in anything she'd touched. I remember one of her French letters going for ten quid which was a lot of money in those days.'

A Nightie to Remember?

Now a nightie had turned up. Its owner was Tommy Videos, a Roman Catholic priest and another of Julie's clients who claimed to have found it in the rubble of Julie's old house on Frontispiece Street. He said it exhibited clear signs of a miraculous imprint of the late woman's body, showing her distinctive directoire knickers, Y-shaped posture and the tattoo above her most secret sanctum which read 'Keep Off the Grass!' Curiously, there was also an image of Julie's face, but it appeared right in the middle of the garment where her abdomen should have been.

The Late Shift

A sceptical Terry Knight, by now minister of his late father's chapel, demanded to see the holy nightdress. After a few pints and a little persuasion he was convinced, announcing that he was 'thirty-five per cent certain' that it was the nightie in which St Julie of Harlow had died. Father Videos even had an explanation for the mysterious face in the stomach: 'Obviously that wrestler had lifted up St Julie's shift over her head so give a good seeing to unimpeded, then at the moment of death her divine radiance had spilled out, imprinting her sacred image onto the nylon for all time.' Was this a divine image or something altogether more prosaic?

Is this the face of St Julie?

The Investigation

By 1996 Knight and Videos' obsession with the relic had led to them being dismissed from the Orthodox Church. Determined to prove the authenticity of the nightdress they offered it up for scientific examination. They removed it from the reliquary – or tea chest – in the crypt of the former Methodist chapel

– now Ed's Discount Carpet Warehouse Harlow – and handed it over to a team of scientists headed by psychic investigator Larry Rice. After a few moments of rigorous examination the team delivered their analysis.

The Theories

Followers of the cult of the nightdress – known as pyjamologists – have suggested that the image was produced by:

1. **A Miracle.** So there.

2. **A so-called 'sexygraph'.** According to this theory the nightie acted as a kind of photographic plate. A chemical reaction between sweat, bodily fluids and cheap Yardley perfume burnt the image of Julie indelibly into the man-made fibre.

3. **Another reaction** between the sweaty mass of Julie's body and her electric blanket. This variation on the second theory was advanced by Japanese pornographer Jai Karate and a nun who experimented disastrously with an inflatable doll filled with hot tea.

4. **Larry Rice's Theory.** 'We didn't have to look too hard', commented the renowned sceptic. 'There were crispy yellow sweat-rings under the armpits, skidmarks and an awful lot of unpleasant stains. The rest of it had been drawn on in biro. Rubbish.'

But Knight and Videos remain convinced of the veracity of their story and like the body of St Julie of Harlow to her nightie, they're sticking to it.

Rice: Crispy

FILE 19

THE ENIGMA OF THE CRYSTAL KNACKERS

In 1988 Essex was agog. The famous County Museum in Chelmsford mounted an extraordinary exhibition which attracted lovers of the bizarre like fifteen year olds to an off-licence. RUBBISH? was an unabashed celebration of fakes and curiosities in which the curators had brought together almost a thousand individual pieces from all over the world.

The Crystal Knackers – what strange and rude secret do they hold?

There was *Ilford Man* – the famous ape skull forgery which had so baffled paleontologists of the late 1920s who thought they had found the missing link between ape and man. In fact it was made from a hollowed-out pineapple with a pair of dentures stuck in it. Also on display was the *Vegetable Fruit* of Bradwell Waterside – a curiosity which fascinated antiquarians who believed it was a rare example of a banana in the shape of a potato. It transpired that it was just a potato.

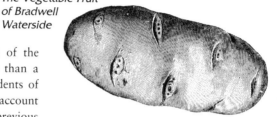

The Vegetable Fruit of Bradwell Waterside

Pubes of Satan

Then there was the curious case of the Devil's Pubes which caused more than a few blushes for the Victorian residents of Burnham-on-Crouch (for a full account and explanation see the authors' previous book *Dirty Mysteries*). Fake laundry lists from Colditz Castle rivalled in their artistry a Raphael painting of the Madonna and Child revealed as a twentieth-century forgery when a connoisseur spotted that the Our Lady was wearing a bikini and flip-flops.

For many though the most extraordinary exhibits were to be found in a little room adjacent to the main display. Here was a group of objects which have baffled experts for many years because they are made of substances such as biscuit for which no definitive dating technique exists. The most amazing exhibit of all was a work of art of 'extraordinary and lewd craftsmanship': The so-called *Crystal Knackers*.

Genesis of the Knackers

Since their first appearance in the early 1970s on a market-stall in Frinton-on-Sea these amazing artifacts have become the stuff of Essex legend. They have been examined in minute detail by experts on paleolithic art, all hoping to find the answer to these questions: who would make such an item and what the hell for?

The Knackers are thought to represent a man's testicles, carved from the rare transparent mineral barriwite. They were found in an archeological dig underneath the Wimpy Bar in Coggeshall*. Of indeterminate age, they may have been broken off a larger phallic shaft, part of a complete genital cluster, the shaft and bishop's hat of which were never found. Superstitious workers on the dig were terrified claiming that the Knackers had evil properties. One of the labourers, Mike MacMansfield, reported that he'd 'got a dose' after handling the strange objects, although when interviewed later he confessed that he'd recently had intimate knowledge of a local girl called Lianne Treason with whom the carnal act was said to be like 'chucking a sausage up the Blackwall Tunnel'.

Curse of the Knackers

But stories of the crystal's hex refused to go away. A window dresser and expert collector, Howard Flies, was called in to examine the mysterious nads early in 1973. After exhaustive work he concluded that:

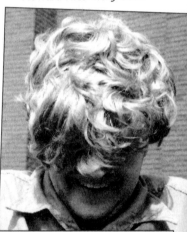

Howard Flies 'itchy bush'

X They were of Paleolithic origin, possibly even pre-dating Stonehenge.

X They had been carved from a single piece of barriwite which may have originated in ancient Mexico.

X He now had the crabs really bad.

---

* This was one of the old-style Wimpy Bars with a Horlicks machine and elderly waitresses and a lurid colour menu with sickly pictures of knickerbocker glories and bizarre looking burgers surrounded by semi-sliced sausages that resembled Elizabethan ruffs. Surely no one ever actually ordered one. They also had those ketchup dispensers made of moulded plastic in the shape of an outsize tomato, but they never solved the problem of what shape to make the brown sauce one. All this went in the fast-food Reformation of 1982 when Wimpy thought they had to move with the times and become like McDonald's, so in came counter service, prepackaged meals and milkshakes made of paper pulp. The thing about the old-style desserts was that they were really complicated to make and this was in the days before they were ready prepared. This prompted you to go in with a schoolfriend like David Clegg and order a banana-boat with extra-whipped cream and then run out before it arrived knowing you'd made somebody do something really difficult and irreversible. Except once you did it and this big fellah with hands like a goalie chased after you and dragged you back by the collar. He stood over you and forced you to eat it even though you now felt so sick with fear you could barely get the spoon into your mouth. The sign outside was in that nice fat lettering not unlike the Goodies writing. All that's gone now. Like the BT logo. What's that mincing stickman with a trumpet all about? And now you're expected to call the Post Office Tower, the Telecom Tower. It's not right. I still can't eat bananas.

Going on to say that he had 'no idea how the little buggers had got into his bush' and that his 'bollocks itched like an amputee's stump' he could only conclude that the crystals were cursed.

Evil of the Knackers

Others too began to notice weird side effects if they handled the artifacts. Popular TV personality Galen Lockjaw who featured the Knackers in *Eh?*, his series about great mysteries, was almost immediately afflicted with the most terrible hair-trigger trouble reporting that he could 'barely get his duds down without shooting his muck'. Later the director of the programme Urko Harryhausen was reported to be suffering from impotence. 'When I were with a girl in the pictures, like, I had a cock-stand like the best of them,' he commented, 'but when we went down the fields it just died.'

Galen Lockjaw – 'shoots his muck'

Planet of the Knackers

A theory advanced by Canadian vulcanologist Lomax Rurapente postulates that the Knackers are carved from transparent material originating from a distant planet which exploded millions of years ago. A theory advanced by Rurapente's psychiatrist postulates that he is 'mad as a shit'.

Terror of the Klackers

So popular was the legend of the Knackers in the early 1970s that they inspired a craze around the children's bumping toy known as Klackers – like two plastic conkers which, if abused, could shatter the wrists of even the hardiest player.

Whatever the theories the crystal Knackers still hold their secret within their see-through scrotal sac. Unfortunately we may never know their real purpose for, like real knackers, they cannot speak. It would be good if they could though, wouldn't it.

FILE 20

SOUTHEND - GATEWAY TO THE STARS

There are some locations that seem to court a sense of mystery inspiring those who visit to ask many questions: the Great Pyramid of Cheops – who built it? Easter Island – who carved the eerie statues? Leicester Forest East Service Station – why does it cost £2.49 for a bowl of Heinz tomato soup? Essex too has its fair share of enigmatic places – perhaps none more so than the popular coastal resort of Southend-on-Sea.

Southend Pier – why so long?

There are those who believe that there is more to this seemingly ordinary, run-down town than candy floss and plates of seaside rock got up to look like bacon and eggs.

Rolf

Aside from the obvious question of who in their right mind would actually want to go to Southend, there are other, more subtle queries that need to be addressed. One man in particular – self-styled cosmologist and amateur gynaecologist 'Dr' Rolf von Blessyou – has developed a complete unifying theory extrapolated from his observations made over a number of years. If correct, his ideas may force us to re-evaluate not only Southend but the very nature of the seaside itself.

"Dr" Rolf von Blessyou

On

Von Blessyou currently holds the chair in Outer Space Studies at Shenfield Metropolitan University. He first came to popular attention in 1979 with his bestseller *Swimming Baths of the Gods* which claimed that the majority of the UK's municipal pools were in fact relics of an ancient civilisation which pre-dated the Romans by thousands of years. His reputation took something of a bashing and the theory became rather discredited after his humiliation on the Russell Harty Show by fellow guests Rod Hull, actress/singer Grace Jones and Emu.

Saturday

Undaunted he began work on a new book after a holiday visit to Southend sowed a seed of unease in his mind. 'I just couldn't understand it. Why was the enchanting children's village Never Never Land only open Saturdays, Sundays and school holidays? Why was that lovely careful replica of the Golden Hind closed, landlocked in a sea of crisp packets and empty cans of pop. And what about that pier – more than a mile long, and it's such an effort to get to the end on that bloody little train and what's there waiting for you? – Madam Rene the fortune-teller and a gents. It just didn't make sense. I knew there had to be more to Southend than an atmosphere of repressed violence and white trash with pushchairs.'

OK?

Von Blessyou began his investigations by writing to Southend Tourist Board assuming the persona of local historian Sir Hilary Bray. He explained that he

Sir Hilary Bray

was researching the history of the resort and wondered whether they would provide him with any primary source material. But all he received in answer was a curt standard letter and a free brochure with money-off coupons to be spent in Pizza Hut. 'It was brusque, almost clinical in its formality. I began to suspect an other-worldly intelligence behind it.' Subjecting the letter to standard tests revealed a shocking and unexpected hidden message. The message read:

'God help us. They have come.'

Von Blessyou had discovered this message by shading lightly over the back of the letter with a 2B pencil. Clearly it was a communication from some fearful Southend resident – desperate for help from the outside world. Von Blessyou knew then that his theory was correct. Aliens were systematically taking over the town, eliminating the real residents and disguising themselves as eighteen-year-old mothers of three and obese car mechanics called Terry. Even the revelation of the message in full, which read:

'Dear Jack, God help us. They have come again and they still can't fix the video. I told you it was better to rent than to buy. Anyway sorry I missed you. See you tonight, OK Love Elaine.'

could not shake Von Blessyou's conviction that something was terribly amiss.

'Obviously whoever had written the note that was resting on top of the brochure had been nobbled by the aliens soon after and forced at blaster-point to neutralise their impassioned plea by burying it in a more mundane message,' he explained.

Did ancient Southenders erect statues to welcome visitors they knew were coming?

Southend is full of inexplicable phenomena

The Last Resort

Von Blessyou decided to act decisively by purchasing a day-return to Southend from Shenfield the next morning. When he arrived he began looking at the formerly innocuous seaside town with a new awareness. 'Everywhere I turned there was evidence that the invasion was already underway.' The facts are as follows:

Southend Pier – long from the other end too

X The bizarre length of the pier becomes understandable when one sees it for what it really is: a vast landing-strip for alien spacecraft. Upon landing the aliens are fed a white antiseptic paste to acclimatise them to the earth's atmosphere. The paste is piped into cornets and served with a chocolatey-brown energy stick inserted into the gooey substance.

X The Cliff Lift which connects the Western Esplanade to the edge of the town centre actually serves as a direct transportation system to move the exhausted pilots to the base of operations beneath Debenhams in the Royals shopping centre. The Lift, disguised as an antiquated vehicular railway is seemingly owned and run by pensioners Joe and Moira who are actually Voorrn and Petrak – already assimilated elder statesmen of the Alien Empire.

The Cliff Lift –
Stairway to
Heaven or
stairway to
Debenhams?

The Golden Hind – careful
replica or filthy breeding
ground?

X The careful replica of the *Golden Hind* is actually an incubation unit and hatchery for alien spawn. Once a popular tourist attraction because of its waxwork Chamber of Horrors this careful replica of Sir Francis Drake's ship was closed by the aliens to keep their filthy breeding secret.

X The adjacent fun park – Peter Pan's Adventure Island – with its gravity defying attractions undoubtedly serves as a training ground for the newly hatched extraterrestrials. The Astro-Turtle and its ilk are in fact heavily disguised spacecraft simulators. The aliens provide their young with an endless supply of tokens so they can have a go on the rides as often as they like.

X Never Never Land is kept shut all week as this is where the aliens live and the cries of visiting children would disturb them. The park is open at weekends during which time the spaceman residents visit relatives who have already landed in other Essex seaside towns. In addition the park situated

The Astro-Turtle – training device for Alien pilots?

Peter Pan's secret hideaway – or roadsign for space-craft?

as it is at the end of the pier is an effective warning that incoming craft have overshot if they approach. Note the instruction given by the sign – Never Never land.

It would be easy to dismiss Von Blessyou's theories as the ramblings of a madman. However, although at first sceptical of his outlandish claims the authors were persuaded after a day trip to Southend left them in an inexplicable state of terror. Attempting to contact Von Blessyou we discovered that, like Laptop Carey, he had completely disappeared. His landlady Courtney Dressage explained that she had been forced to break down his door which was locked from the inside. All that she found within was an unfunny seaside postcard and a half-eaten 99 cornet.

As we walked away from Von Blessyou's Shenfield lodging we quickened our step. Everywhere it seemed there were harried teenage girls clutching toddlers and hard-looking leery men clutching cans of lager although it was only 10.30 in the morning. Suddenly we looked at them in a new and strangely alien light.

CONCLUSION

We have come a long way since our first tentative steps into the county of mystery that Essex proved to be.

We have seen that all aspects of the unexplained are contained within its borders, from the horror of Gossip's, Romford, to the enigma of Cobbler's Mede Rock, from the puzzle of the Crystal Knackers to the awesome terror that is Southend.

But, as we reach the end of our strange journey, one major question seems to stand out over all others – Why is all that is bizarre concentrated in this one little county?

We have heard the testimony of Dixie Quatermass and his theory of aggressive plate tectonics. And Rolf Von Blessyou, who may have paid the ultmate price for his curiosity about alien visitors. And then there is Laptop Carey, the first to identify the heritage of the bizarre in his county of origin.

But who is right, and how does this fit with the ideas outlined in our introduction?

After hours of exhaustive research we have drawn together the threads that form this giant tapestry of strangeness. The cases, each like a cut-off piece of material, seemingly discarded and cast aside, when punched into the whole create a rag-rug of truth. The themes weave throughout like the warp and weft of an Axminster of the Odd which runs the length of the hallway of enquiry and then up the staircase of analysis but doesn't quite reach the base of the banisters of ignorance on either side, and so leaves a tiny area uncovered: the bare floorboards of doubt.

It is on this rickety stairwell that we have attempted to paste the carpet glue of certainty.

Back and to the Left

You may remember that we began by asserting that the outline closely resembled the silhouette of assassinated US president, John Fitzgerald Kennedy. Incredibly if one were to take a magic marker and join together each of the locations mentioned in this book the resulting pattern would closely resemble Kennedy's head after the magic bullet had done its terrible work.

This is clearly a sign that mysteries of Essex share a direct link with a larger, more global network of conpiracy. Now at last we can disclose the astonishing extent of this web of fear.

Teletranscombobulist 'Big' Lee Vincent was often to be seen smoking Marlboro cigarettes, the design of whose packaging exhibits a proven link to far-right white supremacist group the Ku-Klux-Klan. Lee himself was a former member of the National Front, whose members often used to be seen at Gossip's NiteSpot in Romford. The entrance of Gossip's contains a large, badly painted picture of Marilyn Monroe, whose mysterious death is often linked to the assassination of both John and Robert Kennedy. Marilyn was married to Pulitzer-prize winning playwright Arthur Miller, whose autobiography is tantalisingly entitled *Timebends*, a coded reference to the phenomenon of Timeslip described within these pages. Marilyn was also married to quick-tempered baseball star Joe DiMaggio, who is name-checked in the Simon and Garfunkel song 'Mrs Robinson' which says 'where have you gone Joe DiMaggio' – where indeed? Intriguingly a Garfunkels restaurant now stands on the sight once occupied by Corringham Ladies College with its own link to unexplained disappearances via the picnic at Cobbler's Mede Rock. One theory advanced, as we have seen, is that aliens landed at the rock, perhaps in the meaty guise seen by Sir Paul McCartney, a sixties pop compatriot of Simon and Garfunkel. However there is evidence that McCartney himself was abducted and replaced, both in his shoe-lessness on the cover of 'Abbey Road' and the blindingly obvious fact that the man who wrote 'Hey Jude' could not have been responsible for 'Rupert and the Frog Chorus'. McCartney almost married flame-haired actress Jane Asher – a woman as ginger in her own way as *EastEnders* star Patsy Palmer whose image caused such consternation in the household of Juliette Mates. Patsy's *EastEnders'* co-star Wendy Richard once made a record called 'Come Outside' *also in the sixties* with Blue Riband man Mike Berry. Amazingly Berry later joined the staff of TV department store Grace Brothers in Wendy Richard's sitcom *Are You Being Served?* as Mr Lucas's replacement Mr Spooner. Even more incredibly actor Nicholas Smith who played jug-eared boss Mr Rumbold had a bit-part as a Robo-Man in *Doctor Who* – a show which began the day after John F. Kennedy's assassination. But the the adventuring Time Lord finally disappeared from its sacred Saturday teatime slot to be replaced in the schedules by none other than *The Little and Large Show*.

We have it seems, come full-circle. The original subject of our research, predating this project by several months, who we abandoned in favour of the mystery that is Essex, turns out to be at the very centre of that mystery. We can only conclude the man the world knows as Syd Little, is nothing of the kind but is, in fact, the cruel alien emperor of a once proud race which is already invading our planet through their spearhead in Southend.

His partner Eddie knew this and showed us the way, probably at great risk to himself.

So please – if only for Eddie's sake – heed this warning.

Stay away from Essex.

Syd Little and his meat-based allies are laughing at us.

For God's sake, keep watching the pies.

A FINAL WORD FROM OUR RESIDENT SCEPTIC

Rice: This entire book isn't worth the paper it's written on.

Do yourself a favour and put this back on the shelf and buy my new book instead – "The SusseX Files"

Rice: Paper

SELECT BIBLIOGRAPHY

Alderan, Travis, *Are Friends Electric? – The Dull Life of Gary Numan*, Pleasure Principle Press, 1985

Arthur, Neil, *Living on the Ceiling – My Life in Blancmange*, Mange-Tout Press, 1990

Blubber, Toby, *This Means Nothing to Me, Oh Vienna – Midge Ure, A Life*, Monument Press, 1996

Broom, June, *Two Clones Dying – The Unauthorized Biography of the Chuckle Brothers*, Moody and Peg Ltd, 1988

Chesney-Hawkes, Sir Thomas, *Victorian Bastards*, Olsen and Johnsen, 1972
Edwardian Cunts, Hope and Keen, 1973
Neo-Georgian Twats, Bennett and Stevens, 1974

Drums, Tintin, *Cue The Music! – The Mike Mansfield Story*, Carlton Late Night Press, 1992

Dyson, Jeremy and Gatiss, Mark, *Dirty Mysteries*, Hodder and Lunchbox, 1994

Handwriting, Grahame, *The Man With Wet Tights – The Prophecies of Nastidampness*, Looking into the Future Press, 1981

Hoth, Bunty, *Scooby, Yes – Scrappy, No*, Goober and Ghostchaser, 1991

Krakas, Ritz, *Codeword Essex – The Essex Code and its Codewords Decoded*, Fishball and Chrane, 1997

Monkeyshines, Fiachra, *Sing Lofty! – The Don Estelle Story*, Hewlett and Knowles, 1982

Rillington-Place, Sir Linford, *The Valley of Sweets and Other Stories – A Simon Buns Omnibus*, Siegfried and Roy, 1919

Ridgeback, Wednesday, *Churchill Was Made of Olives and Other Conspiracy Theories*, Christopher and Lillicrap, 1992

Sweaters, David, *Standing Proud – The Cheeky Man of Chelmsford, A Rude Legacy in Chalk*, Chelmsford Society for the Promotion of Smut

Tattooine, Ginster, *The League of Nancies – Dashing Queens of Crime*, Godley and Creme, 1982

INDEX